SCHOLASTIC

Morning Jumpstarts: MATH

100 Independent Practice Pages to Build Essential Skills

Marcia Miller & Martin Lee

New York • Toronto • London • Auckland • Sydney
Mexico City • New Delhi • Hong Kong • Buenos Aires

Edited by Mela Ottaiano
Cover design by Michelle H. Kim
Cover photo © DGLimages/iStockphoto
Interior design by Melinda Belter
Interior illustrations by Teresa Anderko, Melinda Belter, Maxie Chambliss, Steve Cox,
James Graham Hale, Mike Moran, and Sydney Wright; © 2013 by Scholastic Inc.
ISBN: 978-0-545-46419-2
Copyright © 2013 by Scholastic Inc.
Published by Scholastic Inc. All rights reserved.
Printed in the U.S.A.
First printing, January 2013.
3 4 5 6 7 8 9 10   40   21 20 19 18 17 16

Contents

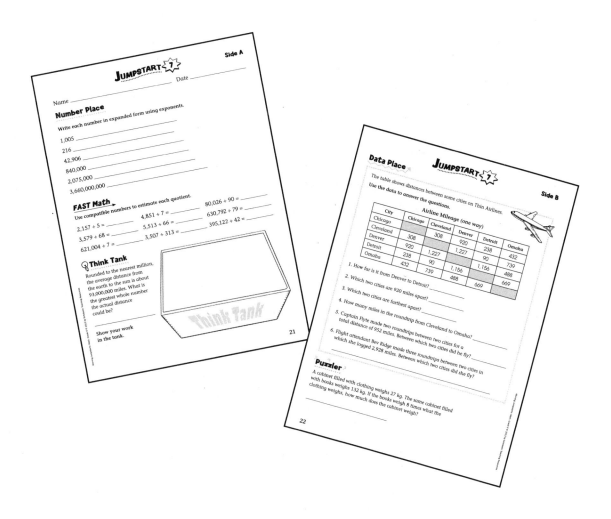

Introduction

In your busy classroom, you know how vital it is to energize students for the tasks of the day. That's why *Morning Jumpstarts: Math, Grade 6* is the perfect tool for you.

The activities in this book provide brief and focused individual practice in grade-level skills students are expected to master. Each Jumpstart is a two-page collection of five activities designed to review and reinforce a range of math skills and concepts students will build throughout the year. The consistent format helps students work independently and with confidence. Each Jumpstart includes these features:

- Number Place
- Fast Math
- Think Tank
- Data Place
- Puzzler

You can use a Jumpstart in its entirety or, because each feature is self-contained, assign sections at different times of the day or to different groups of learners. The Jumpstart activities will familiarize students with the kinds of challenges they will encounter on standardized tests, and provide a review of skills they need to master. (See page 6 for a close-up look at the features in each Jumpstart.)

The Common Core State Standards (CCSS) for Mathematics serve as the backbone of the activities in this book. On pages 7–8, you'll find a correlation chart that details how the 50 Jumpstarts dovetail with the widely accepted set of guidelines for preparing students to succeed in math.

Generally, we have kept in mind the eight CCSS "mathematical practices" that should inform solid math exploration, calculation, and interpretation.

Mathematical Practices

1. Make sense of problems and persevere in solving them.
2. Reason abstractly and quantitatively.
3. Construct viable arguments and critique the reasoning of others.
4. Model with mathematics.
5. Use appropriate tools strategically.
6. Attend to precision.
7. Look for and make use of structure.
8. Look for and express regularity in repeated reasoning.

Morning Jumpstarts: Math, Grade 6 © © 2013 by Scholastic Teaching Resources

How to Use This Book

Morning Jumpstarts: Math, Grade 6 can be used in many ways—and not just in the morning! You know your students best, so feel free to pick and choose among the activities, and incorporate those as you see fit. You can make double-sided copies, or print one side at a time and staple the pages together.

We suggest the following times to present Jumpstarts:

- At the start of the school day, as a way to help students settle into the day's routines.
- Before lunch, as students ready themselves for their midday break.
- After lunch, as a calming transition into the afternoon's plans.
- Toward the end of the day, before students gather their belongings to go home, or as homework.

In general, the Jumpstarts progress in difficulty level and build on skills covered in previous sheets. Preview each one before you assign it to ensure that students have the skills needed to complete them. Keep in mind, however, that you may opt for some students to skip sections, as appropriate, or complete them together at a later time as part of a small-group or whole-class lesson.

Undoubtedly, students will complete Jumpstart activity pages at different rates. We suggest that you set up a "what to do when I'm done" plan to give students who need more time a chance to finish without interruption. For example, you might encourage students to complete another Jumpstart or get started on a math homework assignment.

An answer key begins on page 109. You might want to review answers with the whole class. This approach provides opportunities for discussion, comparison, extension, reinforcement, and correlation to other skills and lessons in your current plans. Your observations can direct the kinds of review or reinforcement you may want to add to your lessons. Alternatively, you may find that having students discuss activity solutions and strategies in small groups is another effective approach.

When you introduce the first Jumpstart, walk through its features with your class to provide an overview before you assign it and to make sure students understand the directions. Help students see that the activities in each section focus on different kinds of skills, and let them know that the same sections will repeat throughout each Jumpstart, always in the same order and position. You might want to work through the first few Jumpstarts as a group until students are comfortable with the routine and ready to work independently.

You know best how to assign the work to the students in your class. You might, for instance, stretch a Jumpstart over two days, assigning Side A on the first day and Side B on the second. Although the activities on different Jumpstarts vary in difficulty and in time needed, we anticipate that once students are familiar with the routine, most will be able to complete both sides of a Jumpstart in anywhere from 10 to 20 minutes.

A Look Inside

Each two-page Jumpstart includes the following skill-building features.

Number Place The first feature on Side A reviews grade-appropriate place-value skills related to whole numbers, decimals, and fractions. Regardless of the particular presentation, students will use their knowledge of place value and their number sense to complete this feature. A solid place-value foundation is essential for success with computation and estimation, and for an overall grasp of numerical patterns and relationships.

Fast Math The second Side A feature addresses necessary grade-level computation skills with the goal of building automaticity, fluency, and accuracy. To work through these exercises, students draw upon their understanding of computation strategies and mathematical properties. In some instances, students will review skills that have been covered previously. This is a good way to keep math skills sharp and to point out to you where revisiting a skill or algorithm may be beneficial.

Think Tank This feature rounds out Side A by offering an original word problem that draws from a wide spectrum of grade-appropriate skills, strategies, and approaches. Some are single-step problems; others require multiple steps to solve. The think tank itself provides a place where students can draw, do computations, and work out their thinking. This is a particularly good section to discuss together, to share solutions, as well as to compare and contrast approaches and strategies. Encourage students to recognize that many problems can be solved in more than one way, or may have more than one solution.

Data Place Every Side B begins with an activity in which students solve problems based on reading, collecting, representing, and interpreting data that is presented in many formats: lists, tables, charts, pictures, and, mostly, in a variety of graphs. In our rapidly changing world, it is essential that students build visual literacy by becoming familiar with many kinds of graphic presentations. This feature presents the kinds of graphs students are likely to encounter online, on TV, and in newspapers and magazines. Some include data from other curriculum areas.

Puzzler Side B always ends with an entertaining challenge: a brainteaser, puzzle, non-routine problem, code, or other engaging task designed to stretch the mind. While some students may find this section particularly challenging, others will relish teasing out trick solutions. This feature provides another chance for group work or discussion. It may prove useful to have pairs of students tackle these together. And, when appropriate, invite students to create their own challenges, using ideas sparked by these exercises. Feel free to create your own variations of any brainteasers your class enjoys.

6

Connections to the Common Core State Standards

As shown in the chart below and on page 8, the activities in this book will help you meet your specific state math standards as well as those outlined in the CCSS. These materials address the following standards for students in grade 6. For details on these standards, visit the CCSS Web site: **www.corestandards.org/the-standards/**.

JS	Ratios & Proportional Relationships			The Number System								Expressions & Equations									Geometry				Statistics & Probability				
	6.RP1	6.RP2	6.RP3	6.NS.1	6.NS.2	6.NS.3	6.NS.4	6.NS.5	6.NS.6	6.NS.7	6.NS.8	6.EE.1	6.EE.2	6.EE.3	6.EE.4	6.EE.5	6.EE.6	6.EE.7	6.EE.8	6.EE.9	6.G.1	6.G.2	6.G.3	6.G.4	6.SP1	6.SP2	6.SP3	6.SP4	6.SP5
1												●		●															
2										●								●			●								
3												●		●				●											
4	●	●	●		●													●			●				●	●	●		
5									●			●	●																
6					●	●			●			●	●		●														
7					●							●				●	●	●											
8					●			●		●		●				●	●	●											
9						●		●	●	●	●										●		●						
10					●											●	●	●							●	●	●	●	●
11			●		●			●					●																
12			●									●		●															
13					●	●										●		●											
14		●			●					●						●		●										●	●
15	●	●			●	●						●				●		●											
16							●	●						●		●		●						●					
17						●							●	●											●	●	●	●	●
18		●				●	●					●				●									●	●		●	●
19		●			●											●	●		●			●							
20	●	●	●							●		●	●			●	●	●											
21	●	●	●		●					●		●					●	●											
22		●	●	●	●					●		●				●	●	●			●								
23				●				●			●	●																	
24					●	●			●			●													●	●	●	●	●
25				●	●	●	●	●	●		●					●	●	●											

Morning Jumpstarts: Math, Grade 6 © 2013 by Scholastic Teaching Resources

Connections to the Common Core State Standards

JS	6.RP.1	6.RP.2	6.RP.3	6.NS.1	6.NS.2	6.NS.3	6.NS.4	6.NS.5	6.NS.6	6.NS.7	6.NS.8	6.EE.1	6.EE.2	6.EE.3	6.EE.4	6.EE.5	6.EE.6	6.EE.7	6.EE.8	6.EE.9	6.G.1	6.G.2	6.G.3	6.G.4	6.SP.1	6.SP.2	6.SP.3	6.SP.4	6.SP.5
26						•		•	•			•	•	•		•	•	•											•
27						•	•	•				•	•	•	•	•	•	•	•		•							•	•
28						•	•	•				•	•	•		•	•											•	•
29					•	•	•	•				•									•								
30			•		•		•	•	•	•	•	•	•	•	•	•							•						
31					•		•			•		•				•	•		•						•	•	•	•	•
32					•		•		•	•		•	•	•	•	•	•				•				•	•			•
33		•	•			•			•			•	•	•	•	•			•		•								
34						•	•	•		•		•	•	•	•	•	•				•	•			•	•	•	•	•
35								•	•	•		•	•	•	•	•	•		•	•					•	•	•		•
36	•	•	•	•	•		•			•		•	•	•	•	•													
37					•		•	•								•	•	•			•				•	•	•		•
38					•			•	•	•						•	•	•							•	•	•		•
39	•	•			•			•	•	•	•					•	•	•		•									
40								•	•			•	•	•	•	•	•				•				•	•		•	•
41	•	•	•							•		•									•								
42	•	•	•		•	•	•			•		•				•	•	•	•	•				•					
43	•	•	•			•		•								•	•	•	•					•					
44	•	•	•					•	•	•					•	•	•		•	•									
45	•	•	•			•	•	•					•	•							•	•		•	•	•		•	•
46	•	•	•			•	•								•	•	•	•	•		•							•	•
47	•		•		•		•		•				•			•	•	•			•				•	•	•	•	
48	•		•			•	•		•	•	•			•		•	•	•											
49	•		•		•	•									•	•	•	•		•	•								
50	•		•	•	•	•								•		•	•	•							•	•	•	•	•

8

Morning Jumpstarts: Math, Grade 6 © 2013 by Scholastic Teaching Resources

Name _____ Date _____

Number Place

Write the number that is 1,000,000 *more*.

352,350 _____   5,802,387 _____

2,307,122,050 _____   19,662,000,000 _____

Write the number that is 1,000,000 *less*.

8,500,000 _____   1,005,555,799,000 _____

500,020,000 _____   7,000,500,000 _____

FAST Math

Compute. Use the properties of addition and multiplication to help you find shortcuts.

$5 + 3^2 + 0 + 5 =$ _____

$1 \times 6^1 + 5 + 0 =$ _____

$3 \times (9 + 7 + 1) =$ _____

$2^1 + 0 + (4 \times 8) + 8 =$ _____

Think Tank

Ellie is numbering her 150-page scrapbook. How many times will she write the digit 4?

_____

Show your work in the tank.

Data Place

The table below shows results of a survey on favorite music groups. But some of the table is blank.

Use the clues to help you fill in the table.

• Twelve students chose Loud Enough.

• The Bugs got the most votes.

• Half as many who voted for Squash voted for Bunny and Hare.

• Fifty-six people took the survey

Music Group	Tally	Number
	ЖЖ ЖЖ II	
		8
		20
	ЖЖ ЖЖ ЖЖ I	

Puzzler

Use each digit from 1–9 to form three addends whose sum is 999.

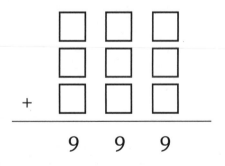

Morning Jumpstarts: Math, Grade 6 © 2013 by Scholastic Teaching Resources

Name _____ Date _____

Number Place

Write the place of the underlined digit.

20,9̲58,007,000 _____

36̲2,004,185 _____

300,2̲64,000,002 _____

1̲5,000,040,312 _____

8,053̲,039,501,000 _____

74,0̲68,289,040 _____

FAST Math ➤

Use all the digits in the box each time
to solve the riddles.

| 2 9 4 3 6 7 5 |

| The sum of these two numbers is 10,089. What are the numbers? | The difference between these two numbers is 7,533. What are the numbers? |

💡 Think Tank

What is the area of the
community garden?

_____

**Show your work
in the tank.**

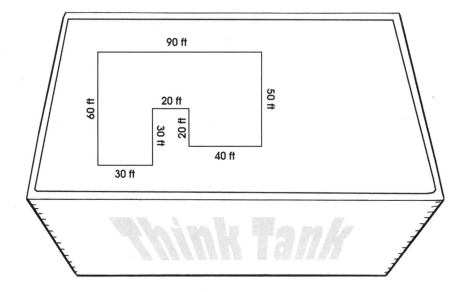

Data Place

The table shows average daily high temperatures in degrees Fahrenheit for some U.S. cities.

Use the data to answer the questions.

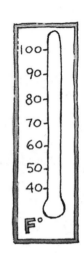

City	January	July
Anchorage, AK	22°	65°
Phoenix, AZ	65°	104°
Boston, MA	37°	82°
Seattle, WA	46°	75°

1. Which city's high winter temperature is about one-third

   of Phoenix's high winter temperature? _____

2. It is the middle of July and the temperature is 10° higher than it is on a typical day

   in Anchorage. Which city are you likely in? _____

3. Which city has the greatest difference between its

   January and July high temperatures? _____

Puzzler

The signs are how they look from the rearview mirror of a car.

Write the words that the mirror reflects.

_____

_____

_____

12

Name _____ Date _____

Number Place

Write each number in standard form.

three hundred billion ten _____

fifty-nine billion one hundred thirty _____

six hundred six billion _____

thirty-two trillion one hundred four _____

FAST Math ▸

Use mental math to find each product.

$4 \times 90 =$ _____ $50 \times 600 =$ _____ $7 \times 40,000 =$ _____

$7 \times 7,000 =$ _____ $10^2 \times 80 =$ _____ $10^2 \times 9,000 =$ _____

$60 \times 800 =$ _____ $30 \times 10^3 =$ _____ $70 \times 40,000 =$ _____

$500 \times 10^3 =$ _____ $50 \times 10^4 =$ _____ $10^1 \times 10^3 =$ _____

💡 Think Tank

Ruth looks at a barnyard picture showing pigs, cows, and hens. She counts 17 heads and 56 legs. How many hens are in the picture?

_____

Show your work in the tank.

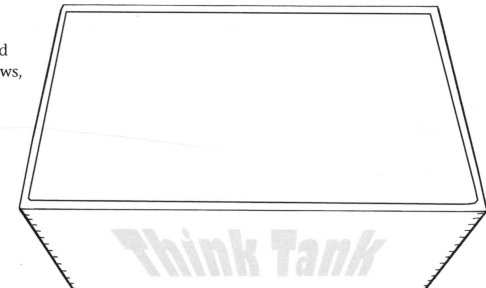

Data Place

Sixth grade students were asked to name their favorite kinds of books. The circle graph shows the results.

Use the data to answer the questions.

1. What fraction of the students chose fantasy?

   _____

2. What fraction chose neither sports nor mystery?

   _____

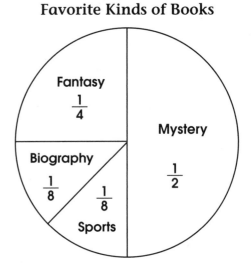

Favorite Kinds of Books

3. Which two kinds of books together got $\frac{3}{4}$ of the votes?

   _____

4. There are 56 students in the 6th grade. What if 10 fewer voted for mystery and

   chose biography instead? How many votes would mystery then get in all? _____

   How many votes for biography? _____

Puzzler

In the magic square, the sum of the numbers in each row, column, and diagonal is the same. This magic sum is the year the first person landed on the moon!

Complete the magic square.

387		383		408
393	405		397	
399	382	395	407	
409		396		392
381		406	390	

14

Name _____ Date _____

Number Place

Complete the table.

Number	Millions	Thousands	Hundreds
1,700,000	1.7	1,700	17,000
8,000,000			80,000
1,800,000,000			
25,000,000,000		25,000,000	
34,500,000			

FAST Math

Estimate the sum by rounding to the greatest place of the least number.

1,825	5,226	29,341	1,574
3,079	468	8,254	60,327
+ 4,255	+ 8,375	+ 473	+ 5,552

Think Tank

Henry rode his bike 5 miles in 25 minutes. What was his average speed in miles per hour?

_____

At that rate, how far does Henry ride in half an hour?

_____

Show your work in the tank.

Morning Jumpstarts: Math, Grade 6 © 2013 by Scholastic Teaching Resources

Data Place

Use the graph about car sales to answer the questions.

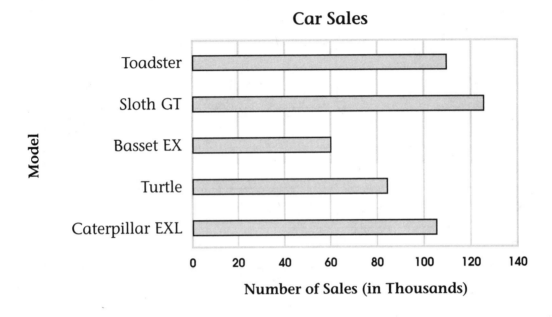

Car Sales

Model

Toadster
Sloth GT
Basset EX
Turtle
Caterpillar EXL

0   20   40   60   80   100   120   140

Number of Sales (in Thousands)

1. Which model had the fewest sales? _____

2. Which model had 25,000 more sales than Turtle did? _____

3. Which two models had a difference in sales of 15,000?

_____

4. What is the range of sales for these models? _____

5. What is the mean number of sales for the five models? _____

Puzzler

The block "staircase" shown has three steps.

**Write how many blocks would it take
to build a 20-step staircase.**

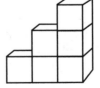

_____

16

Morning Jumpstarts: Math, Grade 6 © 2013 by Scholastic Teaching Resources

Name _____ Date _____

Number Place

Write each power of 10 in standard form.

$10^3 = $ _____ $10^0 = $ _____

$10^7 = $ _____ $10^8 = $ _____

$10^4 = $ _____ $10^1 = $ _____

$10^2 = $ _____ $10^6 = $ _____

FAST Math

Estimate by rounding each factor to its greatest place.

$31 \times 209 = $ _____ $7 \times 768 = $ _____

$46 \times 542 = $ _____ $84 \times 6{,}441 = $ _____

$57 \times 3{,}299 = $ _____ $610 \times 980 = $ _____

Think Tank

Mike asks Ike for change for a dollar. Ike tells Mike that although he has $1.15 in change, he cannot make change for a dollar. Mike tells Ike that he certainly can. Who is right? Explain.

_____

_____

_____

_____

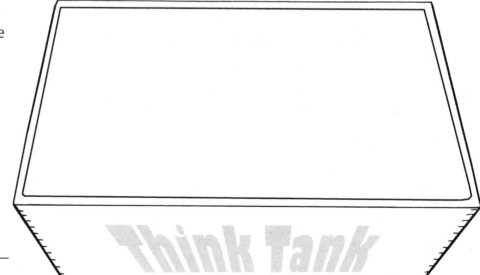

Show your work in the tank.

Data Place

Leah and her brother Ray compared the amount of time each spent on homework one week. The graph shows the results.

Use the data to answer the questions.

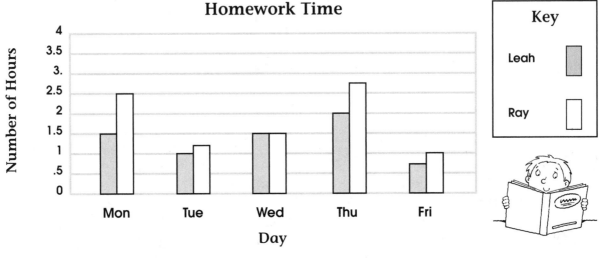

1. How much longer than Leah did Ray work on Monday? _____

2. How much less did Leah work on Friday than she did on Wednesday? _____

3. On which day did the two work for the same amount of time? _____

4. On which day did they work the longest? _____

   How long altogether did they work that day? _____

Puzzler

Try this number trick. Start with *any* five-digit number. But make sure that the difference between the first and last digits is at least 2.

Write your number here _____

- Swap the first and last digits.
- Subtract the smaller number from the larger one.
- Swap the first and last digits.
- Add these two numbers. What is the sum? _____
- Now try the trick with other 5-digit numbers. What do you notice?

Morning Jumpstarts: Math, Grade 6 © 2013 by Scholastic Teaching Resources

Name _____ Date _____

Number Place

Write each as a power of 10.

100 = _____   1 = _____

10,000 = _____   1,000,000 = _____

1,000 = _____   10,000,000 = _____

FAST Math

Find the value of y. Use basic facts to help you.

$240 \div 3 = y$ _____ $280 \div 7 = y$ _____ $4,800 \div 6 = y$ _____

$y = 810 \div 9$ _____ $y = 600 \div 5$ _____ $y = 2,000 \div 40$ _____

Compare. Write **<**, **=**, or **>**.

$36,000 \div 6$ _____ $40,000 \div 8$ $450,000 \div 90$ _____ $2,500 \div 50$

Think Tank

The team orders 4 tacos, a foot-long dog, 2 burgers, 3 sliders, and two of each kind of drink. Coach buys a drink for himself and pays for all with a $100 bill. His change is $28.14. Which drink did he order?

_____

Show your work in the tank.

TAKE-OUT MENU	
Foot-long Dog .. $9.95	Juice $2.59
Burger $7.79	Soda $1.75
Taco .... $4.95 each	Milk $1.50
Pork Slider ...... $3.95 each	Tea............ $1.00

Data Place

Use the calendar to answer the questions.

APRIL

SUN	MON	TUE	WED	THU	FRI	SAT
			1	2	3	4
5	6	7	8	9	10	11
12	13	14	15	16	17	18
19	20	21	22	23	24	25
26	27	28	29	30		

What are the dates?

1. Five in a row have a mean of 21. _____

2. Three in a row have a product of 1,716. _____

3. Two in a row have a product of 812 and a sum of 57. _____

4. Two are prime numbers with a product of 493. _____

5. Three consecutive odd dates have a product of 4,845. _____

_____

Puzzler

Look at the numbers in the box. What do they all have in common?

_____

_____

_____

_____

15	62	37
	26	48
51	84	73
	95	59

Morning Jumpstarts: Math, Grade 6 © 2013 by Scholastic Teaching Resources

Name _____ Date _____

Number Place

Write each number in expanded form using exponents.

1,005 _____

216 _____

42,906 _____

840,000 _____

2,075,000 _____

3,660,000,000 _____

FAST Math ▸

Use compatible numbers to estimate each quotient.

2,157 ÷ 5 = _____   4,851 ÷ 7 = _____   80,026 ÷ 90 = _____

3,579 ÷ 68 = _____   5,513 ÷ 66 = _____   630,792 ÷ 79 = _____

621,004 ÷ 7 = _____   3,507 ÷ 313 = _____   395,122 ÷ 42 = _____

Think Tank

Rounded to the nearest million, the average distance from the earth to the sun is about 93,000,000 miles. What is the greatest whole number the actual distance could be?

_____

Show your work in the tank.

Data Place

The table shows distances between some cities on Thin Airlines.

Use the data to answer the questions.

Airline Mileage (one way)

City	Chicago	Cleveland	Denver	Detroit	Omaha
Chicago		308	920	238	432
Cleveland	308		1,227	90	739
Denver	920	1,227		1,156	488
Detroit	238	90	1,156		669
Omaha	432	739	488	669	

1. How far is it from Denver to Detroit? _____

2. Which two cities are 920 miles apart? _____

3. Which two cities are farthest apart? _____

4. How many miles is the roundtrip from Cleveland to Omaha? _____

5. Captain Flyte made two roundtrips between two cities for a total distance of 952 miles. Between which two cities did he fly? _____

6. Flight attendant Bev Ridge made three roundtrips between two cities in which she logged 2,928 miles. Between which two cities did she fly?

_____

Puzzler

A cabinet filled with clothing weighs 27 kg. The same cabinet filled with books weighs 132 kg. If the books weigh 8 times what the clothing weighs, how much does the cabinet weigh?

_____

Name _____ Date _____

Number Place

Write each in standard form.

$(9 \times 10^4) + (6 \times 10^2)$ _____

$(3 \times 10^5) + (2 \times 10^4) + (7 \times 10^2)$ _____

$(5 \times 10^6) + (4 \times 10^5) + (9 \times 10^3) + (6 \times 10^0)$ _____

$(6 \times 10^8) + (1 \times 10^4) + (8 \times 10^1)$ _____

FAST Math

Find each quotient and remainder.

$5{,}777 \div 34 =$ _____ $72{,}072 \div 72 =$ _____ $400{,}458 \div 186 =$ _____

$1{,}634 \div 15 =$ _____ $36{,}389 \div 82 =$ _____ $88{,}408 \div 514 =$ _____

$2{,}710 \div 759 =$ _____ $28{,}671 \div 57 =$ _____ $113{,}642 \div 364 =$ _____

Think Tank

Consecutive numbers are numbers in counting order. The sum of the squares of four consecutive numbers is 230. What is the sum of the numbers themselves?

_____

Show your work in the tank.

Data Place

Study the coordinate grid to see some places in Tim's town:

A	Coffee Shop	**B**	Fire Station
C	Main Square	**D**	Newsstand
E	Audio Mart	**F**	Parking Garage
G	Bob's Bakery	**H**	Computer City

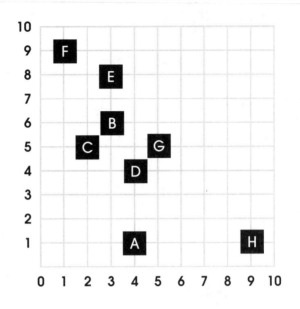

Name the ordered pair for each point.

1. **A** _____   2. **F** _____   3. **H** _____   4. **C** _____

Name the point and the place it represents.

5. (9, 1) _____

6. (4, 4) _____

7. (3, 8) _____

8. (5, 5) _____

Puzzler

Each letter represents a digit.

Find the missing digits in the problem.

$$
\begin{array}{r}
A\,B\,C\,D \\
\times \qquad 4 \\
\hline
D\,C\,B\,A
\end{array}
$$

A = _____   B = _____   C = _____   D = _____

Morning Jumpstarts: Math, Grade 6 © 2013 by Scholastic Teaching Resources

Name _____ Date _____

Number Place

Compare. Write <, =, or >.

788,000 _____ 780,000,000

606,666,000 _____ 606,000,666

87,000,000,000 _____ 970,000,000

fifty million _____ 50,000,000

four hundred four billion _____ 400,000,004

three trillion five hundred million _____ 3,500,000,000

FAST Math ▶

Write the tenth number in each sequence.

0.4, 0.6, 0.8, 1.0, 1.2, 1.4, . . . _____

1.2, 4.2, 9.2, 16.2, 25.2, 36.2, . . . _____

0.1, 0.5, 0.3, 0.7, 0.5, 0.9, . . . _____

💡 Think Tank

The total area of Taiwan is 13,892 square miles. Tajikistan is 41,359 square miles larger. Tanzania's total area is 364,900 square miles. How much smaller than Tanzania is Tajikistan?

_____

Show your work in the tank.

Data Place

In each grid below, locate the points for the ordered pairs. Connect the points in order and then connect the last point to the first one. Then write *isosceles, equilateral,* or *scalene* to describe the triangle you have formed.

1. A (1, 1), B (3, 3), C (7, 1)

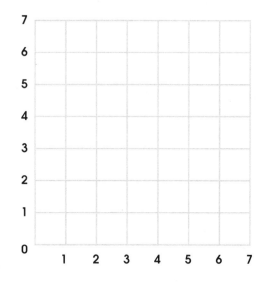

_____

2. D (3, 1), E (1, 7), F (6, 4)

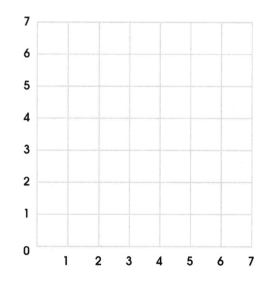

_____

Puzzler

Try this toothpick challenge:
Remove 6 toothpicks
to form two triangles.

Show your answer.

Morning Jumpstarts: Math, Grade 6 © 2013 by Scholastic Teaching Resources

Name _____ Date _____

Number Place

Write the decimal.

eight tenths _____   six hundredths _____

sixty-three hundredths _____   sixteen thousandths _____

nine ten-thousandths _____   one and two hundredths _____

FAST Math ▶

Find each sum or difference.

7 + 8.56 = _____   0.852 + 0.45 + 0.2613 = _____

2.08 + 0.707 = _____   9.3 + 0.4637 + 0.5441 = _____

8 – 2.0476 = _____   0.91 – 0.745 = _____

💡 Think Tank

Rosie bought a painting for $1,000. She sold it for $1,200. Then she bought it back for $1,500 and sold it again for $1,800. In the end, did she make or lose money? How much?

_____

Show your work in the tank.

Data Place

The students in Ms. Bunsen's science class took a quiz today.
The line plot shows their scores.

Use the data to answer the questions.

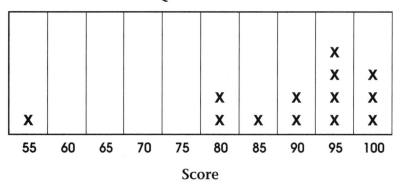

Quiz Scores

Score

1. How many students took the quiz? _____

2. Which score is an outlier? _____

3. Around which score do the data cluster? _____

4. What are the range, mean, median, and mode of the scores?

_____

5. What are the range, mean, median, and mode of the scores *without* the outlier?

_____

Puzzler

1. What do the dates March 16, 1948, February 25, 1950, and August 8, 1964 have in common?

_____

2. What were the *first* three dates in 2012 that have a similar pattern?

_____

Morning Jumpstarts: Math, Grade 6 © 2013 by Scholastic Teaching Resources

Name _____ Date _____

Number Place

Write the value of the variable.

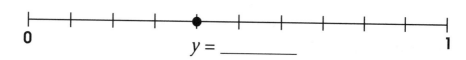

$y =$ _____

$w =$ _____

FAST Math

Estimate the product by rounding each factor to its greatest place.

$4.21 \times 2.3 =$

_____

$6.56 \times 8.8 =$

_____

$9.5 \times 0.85 =$

_____

$83.405 \times 0.63 =$

_____

$15.92 \times 0.96 =$

_____

$9.645 \times 4.1 =$

_____

$93.17 \times 0.92 =$

_____

$15.805 \times 3.46 =$

_____

Think Tank

A meter is approximately 39.37 inches long. To the nearest inch, how long is one meter?

_____

To the nearest foot, how long is one kilometer?

_____

Show your work in the tank.

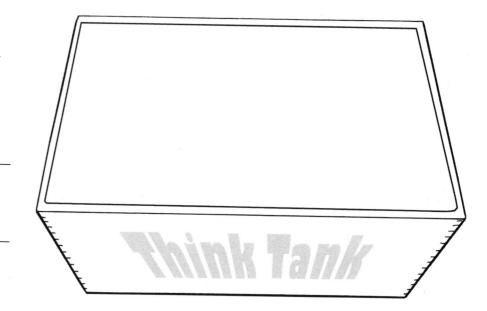

Data Place

The table shows scoring in a football league.

The Bees played the Moths.

Use the clues to fill in the scoreboard.

Touchdown	6 points
Touchdown With Extra Point	7 points
Field Goal	3 points
Safety	2 points

- Each team scored a field goal in the first quarter.

- The Moths led by 1 point at the half.

- The Bees scored a touchdown with an extra point and a field goal in the third quarter. In the fourth quarter, they scored a touchdown and a safety.

- The Moths scored a safety in the third quarter and two touchdowns with extra points in the last quarter.

Quarter	1	2	3	4	Final Score
Bees		6			
Moths					

Puzzler

The bus route from Turtle to Dove is shown below.
How many trips between stops are possible?

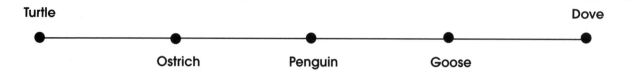

Turtle   Ostrich   Penguin   Goose   Dove

Name _____ Date _____

Number Place

Write each in standard form.

12 hundred thousandths _____

60 and 9 hundredths _____

47 ten-thousandths _____

7 thousand and 22 thousandths _____

FAST Math →

Find each product mentally.

$10^1 \times 0.02 =$ $10^1 \times 0.063 =$ $10^2 \times 0.04 =$ $10^2 \times 0.2 =$

_____   _____   _____   _____

$10^1 \times 0.007 =$ $10^3 \times 0.003 =$ $10^3 \times 3.024 =$ $10^2 \times 5.047 =$

_____   _____   _____   _____

💡 Think Tank

The weight of a bag of chips is labeled 6.5 ounces. This weight has been rounded to the nearest tenth of an ounce. What is the least that the actual weight of the bag could be?

_____

Show your work in the tank.

Data Place

The map shows the mileage from Juniper to Cranberry.
Lena left Juniper with 14 gallons in her car's gas tank.
She ran out of gas 5 miles past Huckleberry.
How many miles per gallon did Lena's car get on this trip?

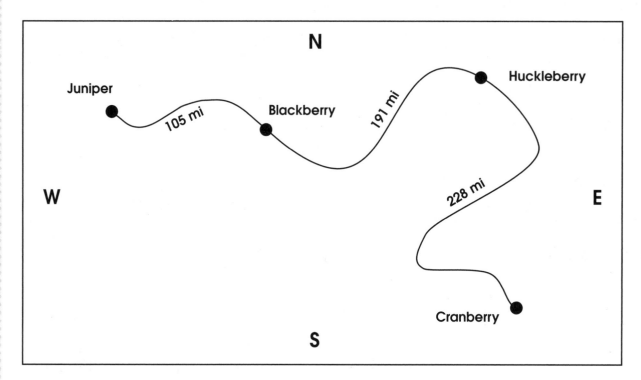

Puzzler

Yu wants to place 10 small round tables along the four walls of a square room so that each of the walls has the same number of tables.

Draw a sketch to show how he can do this.

32

Morning Jumpstarts: Math, Grade 6 © 2013 by Scholastic Teaching Resources

Name _____ Date _____

Number Place

Round each number to the nearest 1,000 *and* 100,000.

Number	Nearest 1,000	Nearest 100,000
389,900		
1,844,938		
24,061,562		

FAST Math →

Divide.

$$100 \overline{)\,0.17}\qquad 22\overline{)\,13.2}\qquad 4\overline{)\,8.792}\qquad 0.1\overline{)\,237}$$

💡 Think Tank

Jake gets the oil changed in his car every 3,500 miles. He had his last oil change done at 34,792.4 miles. What will his car's odometer read when he has his next oil change?

_____

Show your work in the tank.

Morning Jumpstarts: Math, Grade 6 © 2013 by Scholastic Teaching Resources

Data Place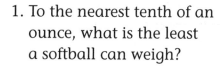

The table shows official weights, in ounces, of some balls for sporting events.

Use the data to answer the questions.

Ball	Weight Range
softball	6.25–7.0
squash	0.821–0.912
tennis	2.0–2.06
croquet	15.75–16.25
volleyball	9.17–9.88
table tennis	0.085–0.09

1. To the nearest tenth of an ounce, what is the least a softball can weigh?

   _____

2. To the nearest tenth, how heavy can a volleyball be?

   _____

3. In which sport can a ball weighing 16 ounces be used? _____

4. Can an official tennis ball weigh 2.1 ounces? _____

5. Which ball weighs about $\frac{1}{10}$ of what a squash ball weighs? _____

Puzzler

Use the numbers 40, 4, and 162 to fill in the blanks in the sentences below in a way that makes sense. Then answer the question.

All _____ students in the sixth grade are going by bus to the play.

Will _____ buses be enough if each bus can take _____ students?

_____

_____

34

Morning Jumpstarts: Math, Grade 6 © 2013 by Scholastic Teaching Resources

Name _____ Date _____

Number Place

Round to the place of the underlined digit.

30,9̲48,007 _____   92,807.04̲5 _____

1,286,000.3̲72 _____   4,000,04̲0,706 _____

8,726,739.02̲83 _____   5,528,90̲8,282 _____

FAST Math ▶

Divide.

$0.001\overline{)0.8}$ $0.01\overline{)1.56}$ $0.4\overline{)0.76}$ $0.8\overline{)0.5}$

Compare. Write **<**, **=**, or **>**.

7 ÷ 8 _____ 1   14.3 ÷ 8 _____ 1   41.1 ÷ 0.99 _____ 1

💡 Think Tank

Carmela's room is a rectangle. Its length is 5.5 yards and its width is 12.3 feet. It has a 9.25-foot ceiling. What is the perimeter of her room?

_____

Show your work in the tank.

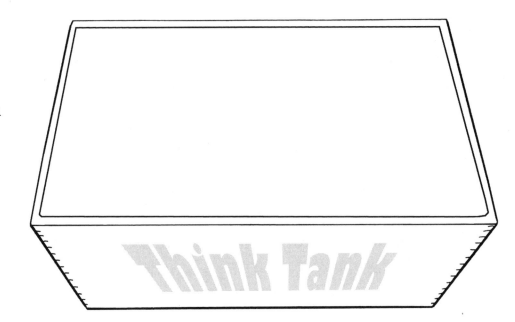

Side B

Data Place

Students were asked to name their favorite T-shirt color. The table shows the results of the survey.

Make a double bar graph to display the data.

Color	Girls	Boys
White	4	7
Blue	8	8
Red	14	13
Green	7	5
Black	9	10

Favorite T-Shirt Colors

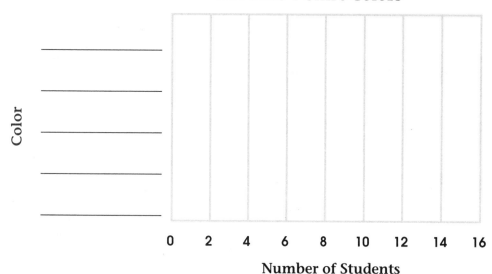

Color

0 2 4 6 8 10 12 14 16

Number of Students

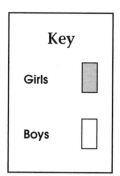

Key

Girls

Boys

Describe what your graph shows. _____

_____

Puzzler

Finn is a fussy eater. Among the foods he will eat are corn, sprouts, beef, and muffins. He will never eat tuna, taco, cheese, or ravioli. Which will he eat—a pancake or a biscuit? _____

Explain. _____

_____

Morning Jumpstarts: Math, Grade 6 © 2013 by Scholastic Teaching Resources

Name _____ Date _____

Number Place

Round to the greatest nonzero place.

0.047 _____   9.807 _____

0.00872 _____   44.8123 _____

6,727.39 _____   0.00526 _____

FAST Math →

Divide.

$2.1\overline{)0.063}$ $9\overline{)0.099}$ $0.2\overline{)0.03}$ $0.032\overline{)0.8}$

💡 Think Tank

Dean hiked 22.8 kilometers.
Dawn hiked 0.6 as far.
How much farther than
Dawn did Dean hike?

_____

Show your work
in the tank.

Data Place

One way to rate baseball players is by comparing their batting averages. To compute a player's batting average, you divide hits by times at bat. Batting averages are generally rounded to three decimal places and do not have a zero before the decimal point.

Complete this batting average table. Then answer the questions.

Player	Hits	At-bats	Batting Average
Jackson	5	40	
Ruiz		90	.300
Morita	46		.250
Hunter		120	.400
Sullivan	26	60	

1. Which player has gotten a hit every 4 at-bats? _____

2. Which has gotten a hit every 2 out of 5 times at bat? _____

3. Sullivan wants to get his average up to .500.
   How many hits will he need in his next 10 at-bats? _____

Puzzler

Use the digits within the box *once* each to complete every number sentence.

3	7	8	1	4

1. ☐ ☐ ☐ – ☐ ☐ = 53

2. ☐ ☐ × ☐ ☐ + ☐ = 3,355

3. ☐ ☐ × ☐ ☐ ☐ = 17,808

Morning Jumpstarts: Math, Grade 6 © 2013 by Scholastic Teaching Resources

Name _____ Date _____

Number Place

Solve.

I am the largest number in ten-thousandths that rounds to 0.683.

What number am I? _____

I am the smallest number in thousandths that rounds to 124.76.

What number am I? _____

FAST Math

Complete.

28 + 8 = 4(___ + 2)

5(3 + ___) = 15 + 40

56 – 35 = ___ (8 – 5)

21 + 7 = 7(3 + ___)

36 – 8 = 4(___ – 2)

3(11 + 15) = 33 + ___

Think Tank

Lefty and Pete divided 724.9 meters of fencing into 100 equal sections. How long is each section?

_____

Show your work in the tank.

Data Place

Use the diagram to answer the questions.

1. How many stars are common to the circle and square, but not the triangle?

   _____

2. How many stars are common to the circle and triangle, but not the square?

   _____

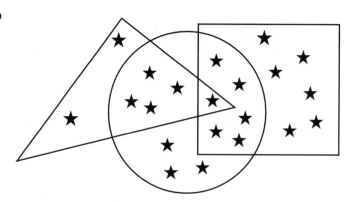

3. How many stars are common to all three figures? _____

4. How many stars are in only one of the three figures? _____

Puzzler

Look at the drawing at the left. One picture in the row shows that drawing in the same position. Circle it.

1.

2.

Name _____ Date _____

Number Place

Find the greatest common factor (GCF) of each set of numbers.

8, 24 _____   15, 35 _____

12, 18 _____   6, 9, 12 _____

5, 12, 14 _____   39, 104 _____

What two numbers between 10 and 20 have 6 as their GCF? _____

What two numbers between 18 and 30 have 8 as their GCF? _____

FAST Math

Round to the nearest whole number to estimate each sum or difference.

$9\frac{7}{8} - \frac{4}{5} =$ _____ $\frac{9}{10} + 1\frac{5}{7} =$ _____ $8\frac{1}{8} + 5\frac{1}{6} =$ _____

$2\frac{3}{4} + \frac{1}{6} =$ _____ $12\frac{2}{3} - 4\frac{5}{8} =$ _____ $\frac{7}{9} - \frac{5}{8} =$ _____

Think Tank

Remi buys some cashews and $2\frac{1}{4}$ pounds of almonds. He buys $5\frac{1}{8}$ pounds of nuts in all. How many pounds of cashews does he buy?

_____

Show your work in the tank.

Data Place

The line graph shows pizza sales at Vinnie's one week.

Use the data to answer the questions.

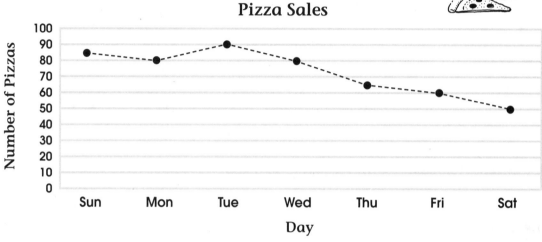

Pizza Sales

1. How many pizzas did Vinnie's sell on Monday? _____

2. Between which two days did the sales drop by 15? _____

3. How many pizzas did Vinnie's sell from Tuesday through Thursday? _____

4. How would you describe the changing pizza sales during the week?

_____

5. What might explain the change? _____

Puzzler

In the magic square, the sum for every row, column, and diagonal is $5\frac{1}{6}$.

Complete the magic square using fractions from the number bank. One fraction is not used.

Number Bank			
$\frac{3}{4}$	$1\frac{1}{12}$	$1\frac{1}{6}$	$1\frac{1}{4}$
$1\frac{5}{12}$	$1\frac{1}{2}$	$1\frac{3}{4}$	$1\frac{11}{12}$

$1\frac{2}{3}$		$1\frac{1}{6}$	$1\frac{7}{12}$
		$\frac{2}{3}$	
$\frac{11}{12}$	$1\frac{5}{6}$		1
	$1\frac{1}{3}$		$\frac{5}{6}$

42

Name _____ Date _____

Number Place

Find the least common multiple (LCM) of each set of numbers.

3, 4 _____   2, 5 _____   40, 16 _____

10, 12 _____   5, 6, 12 _____   8, 9, 10 _____

7, 8, 56 _____   5, 9, 27 _____   8, 13, 52 _____

FAST Math ▸

Find each sum or difference in simplest form.

$\frac{5}{6} - \frac{1}{3} =$ _____ $\frac{3}{8} + \frac{5}{24} =$ _____ $3\frac{7}{8} + 3\frac{1}{2} =$ _____

$\frac{7}{8} - \frac{4}{5} =$ _____ $6 - 4\frac{1}{8} =$ _____ $10\frac{3}{8} - 7\frac{5}{8} =$ _____

$9\frac{1}{12} - 5\frac{3}{8} - 1\frac{3}{4} =$ _____ $15\frac{5}{6} + 12\frac{7}{9} =$ _____

💡 Think Tank

The same number is added to the numerator and denominator of a fraction less than 1. Will the new fraction formed be less than, equal to, or greater than the original one? Explain.

_____

_____

_____

Show your work in the tank.

Data Place

The histogram shows the number of text messages sixth graders sent one Saturday.

Use the data to answer the questions.

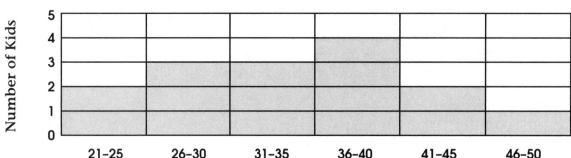

Text Messages Sent

1. How many kids sent between 46 and 50 messages? _____

2. How many kids sent fewer than 36 messages? _____

3. How many more kids sent between 36 and 40 messages than sent between 21 and 25 messages? _____

4. What is the mode of the data? _____ How can you tell?

_____

Puzzler

Use one number from the triangle and one from the circle to answer the questions.

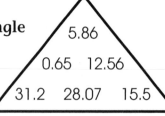

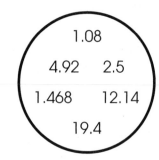

1. Which two numbers have a sum of 13.64? _____

2. Which two numbers have a difference of 11.8? _____

3. Which two numbers have a sum of 18 and a difference of 13? _____

Name _____ Date _____

Number Place

Write whether the fraction is closest to 0, $\frac{1}{2}$, or 1.

$\frac{1}{8}$ _____ $\frac{13}{15}$ _____ $\frac{5}{8}$ _____ $\frac{7}{10}$ _____

$\frac{2}{9}$ _____ $\frac{9}{20}$ _____ $\frac{17}{28}$ _____ $\frac{1}{3}$ _____

Complete. Write a fraction that is equal to or close to $\frac{1}{2}$.

$\frac{n}{11}$ _____ $\frac{n}{15}$ _____ $\frac{9}{n}$ _____ $\frac{n}{9}$ _____

$\frac{n}{27}$ _____ $\frac{4}{n}$ _____ $\frac{n}{21}$ _____ $\frac{15}{n}$ _____

FAST Math

Find each product in simplest form.

$\frac{12}{20} \times \frac{5}{6} =$ _____ $\frac{3}{4} \times \frac{2}{9} =$ _____ $\frac{2}{3} \times 18 =$ _____

$3\frac{1}{7} \times 4\frac{2}{3} =$ _____ $4\frac{1}{6} \times 12 =$ _____ $\frac{5}{9} \times 2\frac{1}{4} =$ _____

Think Tank

The box LaShawni's TV came in measures 6 feet by $4\frac{1}{2}$ feet, by $8\frac{1}{2}$ inches. What is the volume of the box in cubic feet?

_____

Show your work in the tank.

Data Place

Rocco's Tacos is all the rage. After waiting in a long line, you can choose from many one-of-a-kind fillings. And Rocco's prices—hardly rock-bottom!

Use the menu to answer the questions.

Ketchup and Tuna Taco	$15.95
Lamb and Lint Taco	$18.95
Tadpole Taco (add 50¢ for special pond sauce)	$12.50
Stallion and Rice Taco	$15.25
All Desserts (ice cream only)	$8.95
All Sides (rice or beans only)	$6.75
All Drinks	$4.00

1. Sam orders the stallion and rice taco, a side, and a drink. He pays with two $20 bills. What will his change be? _____

2. Ivanka orders the most expensive taco and two sides. She has $15 OFF coupon. Can she also buy a dessert if she has $25? Explain.

   _____

3. Annie spent $30 on her meal, including a $4.05 tip. She ordered three things. What did she order?

   _____

Puzzler

Try this handshake problem.

> Twelve players entered the video game tournament. Each player shook hands with every other player. How many handshakes were there?

Hint: Use simpler numbers and look for a pattern.

Name _____ Date _____

Number Place

Write the number in standard form.

1×10^2 _____ 10^4 _____ $10^3 + 10^2$ _____

3×10^3 _____ 10^6 _____ $5^2 + 10^4$ _____

FAST Math ➡

Rename each unit of measure.

40 ft = _____ yd   114 in = _____ ft   8 gal = _____ qt

80 oz = _____ lb   50 fl oz = _____ c   4 T = _____ lb

Compare. Write **<**, **=**, or **>**.

7 gal _____ 29 qt   7 pt 5 c _____ 19 c   33 pt _____ 16 qt 1pt

10 c _____ 6 pt   15 yd _____ 50 ft   4.5 T _____ 10,000 lb

💡 Think Tank

A freight train is half a mile long. It travels at a speed of 60 mph. It comes to a tunnel that is 1 mile long. How long will it take the train to pass completely through?

_____

Show your work in the tank.

Data Place

Some students at Galileo School have projects on display in the science fair. The graph shows how many students from each grade have their work on display.

Use the data to answer the questions.

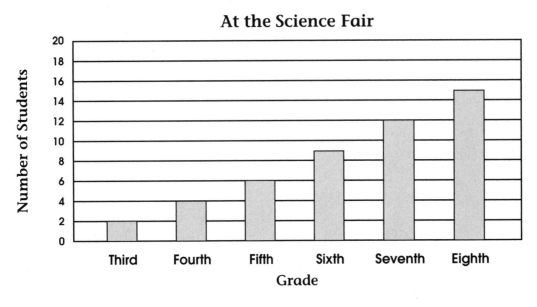

1. How many students have projects on display? _____

2. How many more 7th graders than 5th graders have projects at the fair? _____

3. What fraction of the student scientists are in 8th grade? _____

4. What fraction are in the highest three grades? _____

5. Which two grades together make up $\frac{1}{3}$ of the students with projects on display?

_____

Puzzler

Laura used the following shortcut to quickly find the sum of all numbers from 1 to 10. Study what she did:

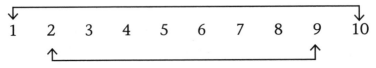

Use Laura's shortcut to find the sum of all numbers from 1 to 100. Explain the method.

_____

_____

48

Name _____   Date _____

Number Place

Solve.

What is the greatest even number you can make that is greater than 5,000,000,000 and less than 6,000,000,000?

_____

What is the greatest number that rounds to 1 billion when rounded to the nearest million?

_____

FAST Math

Rename each unit of measure.

6 cm = _____ m   9.7 km = _____ m   4.8 m = _____ cm

19 g = _____ mg   0.768 L = _____ mL   621 mg = _____ g

Compare. Write <, =, or >.

0.45 m ___ 45 cm   8.8 km ___ 880 m   24 L ___ 240 mL

24 g ___ 240 mg   1.55 kg ___ 1,550 g   3,100 mL ___ 3 L

Think Tank

City A reported 1.45 m of rain. City B reported 139.5 cm of rain. Which city had more rain? Explain.

_____

_____

_____

_____

Show your work in the tank.

Data Place

The information on the gas pumps tells the price per gallon.

Use this price information to answer the questions. Round your answers to the nearest cent.

Regular
$3.49

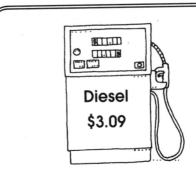

Diesel
$3.09

1. **Greg's car**
   Tank capacity: 18 gal
   Gallons left: 8.6

   Gallons used: _____

   Cost to fill tank with regular gasoline:

   _____

2. **Camille's car**
   Tank capacity: 24 gal
   Gallons left: 4.7

   Gallons used: _____

   Cost to fill tank with diesel gasoline:

   _____

3. Greg has a coupon for $\frac{1}{10}$ off the price of regular. What will it cost to fill the rest of his tank with that discount? _____

Puzzler

Try this penny problem.

Suppose you have 1,000,000 pennies. If you could stack them on top of one other, about how high would the stack reach?

Hint: You don't need to make the whole stack to make a sensible estimate.

Name _____ Date _____

Number Place

Compare. Write **<**, **=**, or **>**.

585,500,000 _____ 585,005,000

300,000,099,000 _____ 300,001,000,000

1,000,000,370,000 _____ one trillion thirty-seven thousand

four hundred fifty trillion _____ 450,000,000,000

FAST Math →

Solve for *n*.

$\frac{1}{2} \div \frac{1}{4} = n$ _____

$\frac{2}{5} \div \frac{1}{10} = n$ _____

$\frac{6}{8} \div \frac{3}{8} = n$ _____

$n = \frac{2}{5} \div \frac{2}{5}$ _____

$n = \frac{9}{10} \div \frac{6}{7}$ _____

$\frac{1}{8} \div \frac{1}{5} = n$ _____

$n = \frac{2}{9} \div \frac{1}{3}$ _____

$n = \frac{6}{13} \div \frac{3}{26}$ _____

$\frac{1}{11} \div \frac{1}{6} = n$ _____

💡 Think Tank

A cubic foot of water weighs $62\frac{1}{2}$ pounds. What is the weight of $5\frac{1}{3}$ cubic feet of water?

_____

Show your work in the tank.

Morning Jumpstarts: Math, Grade 6 © 2013 by Scholastic Teaching Resources

Data Place

Frank's Fruits is an online fruit delivery business.

Place your order and wait for the doorbell to ring.

Use the price list to fill the food orders.

Frank's Fabulous Prices	
Peaches	$1.28/lb
Bananas	$.79/lb
Grapes	$1.99/lb
Limes	5 for $1
Apples	$1.40/lb

1.5 lb apples
2 lb bananas
15 limes

3.5 lb apples
$\frac{3}{4}$ lb peaches
$\frac{1}{2}$ doz. limes

1. Total price: _____

2. Total price: _____

Puzzler

The cake at the right is in the shape of a rectangle.

1. Using 3 straight cuts, what is the greatest number of pieces of cake you can make?

_____

2. What is the greatest number of pieces you can make with 4 straight cuts?

_____

Morning Jumpstarts: Math, Grade 6 © 2013 by Scholastic Teaching Resources

Name _____ Date _____

Number Place

Write each of the following.

an expression with *factors* 3 and *y* _____

an expression with a *coefficient* of 7 _____

an expression for a number decreased by 6 _____

an expression that is the *quotient* of *w* and 4 _____

an expression for 10 more than a number _____

FAST Math →

Find each quotient.

$9 \div \frac{3}{7} =$ _____ $27 \div \frac{3}{5} =$ _____ $\frac{7}{15} \div 42 =$ _____

$84 \div 5\frac{1}{4} =$ _____ $3\frac{1}{2} \div \frac{1}{3} =$ _____ $6 \div 2\frac{1}{4} =$ _____

$3\frac{1}{4} \div 1\frac{1}{2} =$ _____ $5\frac{1}{7} \div 2\frac{1}{7} =$ _____ $4\frac{4}{5} \div 1\frac{1}{5} =$ _____

💡 Think Tank

Sixty-four kids play in a single-elimination chess tournament. That means that one loss knocks a player out of the competition. How many games will it take to determine the winner of the chess tournament?

_____

Show your work in the tank.

Data Place

The map of Canine County is graphed on a coordinate grid.

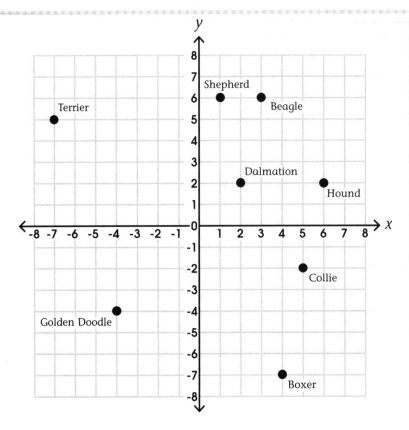

Use the information on the grid to answer the questions.

1. In which quadrant will you find each town?

   Beagle _____   Terrier _____   Golden Doodle _____

2. What are the coordinates for each town?

   Shepherd _____   Collie _____   Hound _____

3. Which town is located at (4, –7)? _____

   In which quadrant is that town? _____

Puzzler

Place as many smiley faces as you can in the grid without getting three in a row vertically, horizontally, or diagonally.

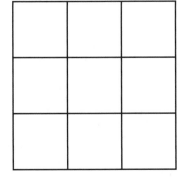

54

Morning Jumpstarts: Math, Grade 6 © 2013 by Scholastic Teaching Resources

Name _____ Date _____

Number Place

Write the value of the variable.

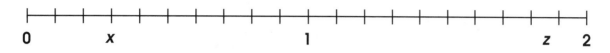

$X =$ _____ $Z =$ _____

FAST Math

Find the range, mean, median, and mode for each set of numbers.

| 3 | 8 | 7 | 12 | 6 | 8 | 14 | 8 | 6 |

range = _____   mean = _____   median = _____   mode = _____

| 62 | 44 | 78 | 57 | 59 |

range = _____   mean = _____   median = _____   mode = _____

Think Tank

On her math tests, Shonda scored 82 once, 85 six times, 90 seven times, and 94 four times. What are the range, mean, median, and mode of her test scores?

_____

_____

_____

_____

Show your work in the tank.

Data Place

The table shows heights, in inches, of students in Mr. Tahl's class.

Make a histogram to display the data.
Give the graph a title.

Height (in Inches)	Frequency
49–52	2
53–56	3
57–60	4
61–64	7
65–68	3
69–72	1

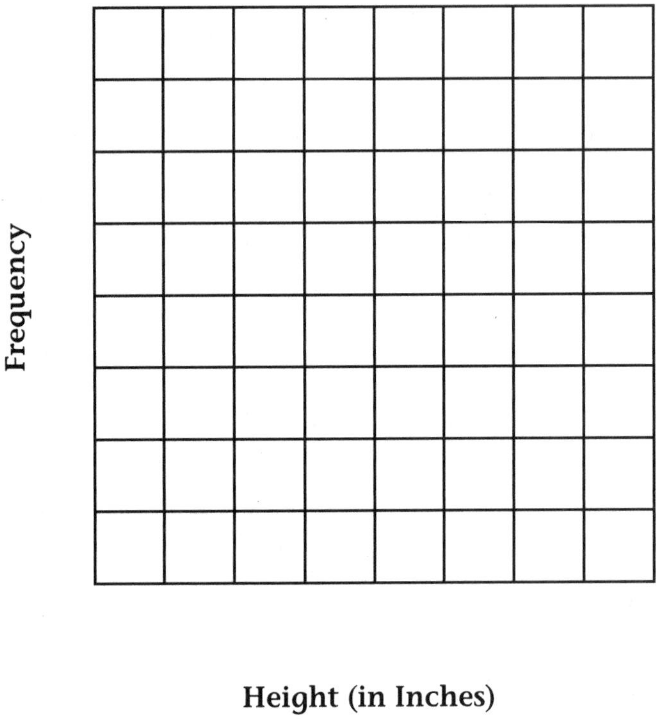

Frequency

Height (in Inches)

Puzzler

Here is a pattern that folds to form a number cube. What are the sums of the numbers on opposite faces of that cube?

_____

_____

_____

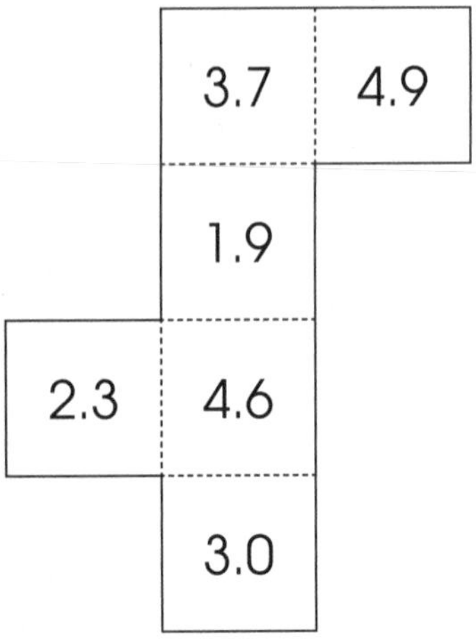

3.7	4.9

1.9

2.3	4.6

3.0

Name _____ Date _____

Number Place

Write the missing numbers.

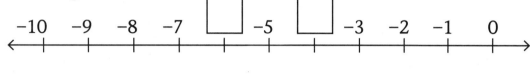

$$-10 \quad -9 \quad -8 \quad -7 \quad \boxed{} \quad -5 \quad \boxed{} \quad -3 \quad -2 \quad -1 \quad 0$$

$$-10 \quad -9 \quad \boxed{} \quad -7 \quad -6 \quad -5 \quad -4 \quad -3 \quad \boxed{} \quad -1 \quad 0$$

FAST Math

Find the range, mean, median, and mode for each set of numbers.

$2.03	$2.46	$2.35	$2.35	$2.91

range = _____   mean = _____   median = _____   mode = _____

$3\frac{1}{2}$	$\frac{5}{8}$	$\frac{3}{4}$	$1\frac{1}{8}$	$2\frac{3}{8}$

range = _____   mean = _____   median = _____   mode = _____

Think Tank

Ted opened his social studies textbook. When Bo asked him to what pages his book was opened, he answered that the product of the facing pages was 87,912. To what pages did Ted open his book?

_____

Show your work in the tank.

Data Place

The map of the sea floor is graphed on a coordinate grid. Each letter on the grid marks the location of a sunken ship.

Each small square on the grid has an area of 1 mi².

Use the grid to answer the questions.

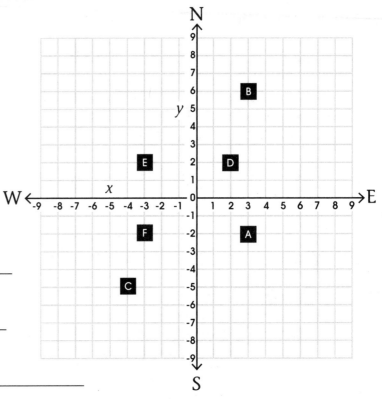

1. Which ship is 6 miles west of ship A? _____

2. Which ship is 5 miles east of ship E? _____

3. Which ship is 7 miles west, 11 miles south of ship B? _____

4. Which ship is 6 miles east, 4 miles north of ship E? _____

5. Which ship is directly northeast of ship F? _____

Puzzler

The six bags below contain either coffee, tea, or cocoa. Only one bag contains tea. There is twice as much coffee as cocoa. What is the weight of the bag that holds the tea? _____

6 lb

7 lb

9 lb

5 lb

3 lb

4 lb

Morning Jumpstarts: Math, Grade 6 © 2013 by Scholastic Teaching Resources

Name _____ Date _____

Number Place

Write the integer that represents each of the following:

a loss of $5 dollars _____

an increase in altitude of 400 feet _____

a dive to 75 feet below sea level _____

a rise in temperature of 6 degrees _____

FAST Math

Write each expression as an algebraic expression. Use *n* as the variable.

a number increased by 7 _____

a number decreased by 2.8 _____

eight more than a number squared _____

the product of a number and 12 _____

Think Tank

Li visited the city. First, she spent one-fourth of her money on breakfast in the train station. Then she spent one-half of what she had left on a train ticket. When she got to the city, she spent one-half of what remained on a taxi to the museum, where she examined her finances over a $2 iced tea. She had only $5.50 left! How much money did Li have with her when she started the day?

_____

Show your work in the tank.

Data Place

Mia is training to run a 5-kilometer race. The graph shows the distances she ran during one week of training.

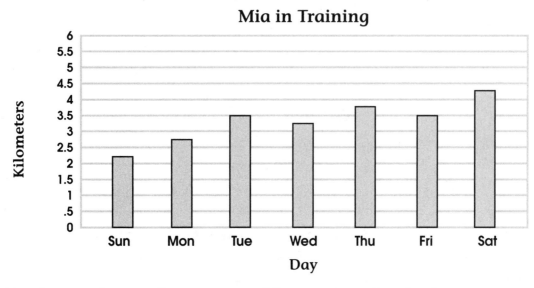

Mia in Training

Use the graph to make up reasonable questions that fit the answers below.

1. **A:** Wednesday and Thursday

   Q: _____

2. **A:** 0.5 kilometers

   Q: _____

3. **A:** 2 kilometers

   Q: _____

Puzzler

Draw a line segment across the clock so that the sums of the numbers on both sides of the line segment are the same.

What is that sum? _____

Name _____ Date _____

Number Place

What inequality is shown? Use *n* as the variable.

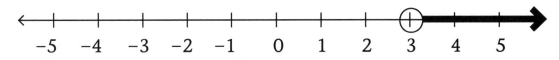

_____

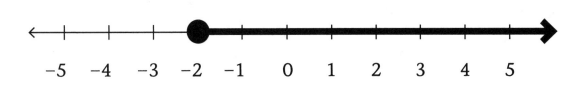

_____

FAST Math

Write each expression as an algebraic expression. Use *n* as the variable.

3 more than twice a number _____

three times a number decreased by 4^2 _____

5 less than twice a number _____

the sum of 8.5 and 2.5 times a number _____

a squared number multiplied by 45 _____

Think Tank

Jack weighs *n* pounds. He carries two packages. One weighs 10 pounds, the other, *d* pounds. Write an expression for the total weight, in pounds, of the two packages.

_____

Show your work in the tank.

Data Place

The line plot shows the shoe sizes of all the members of the school baseball team.

Shoe Sizes

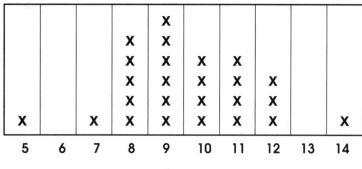

| 5 | 6 | 7 | 8 | 9 | 10 | 11 | 12 | 13 | 14 |

Score

The team's equipment manager made the line plot from data she collected and recorded in a frequency table.

Show what that table would look like. Then summarize what the data shows.

_____

_____

_____

Shoe Size	Tally	Frequency

Puzzler

This hexagon consists of six line segments. How many new line segments can you draw to connect all the vertices?

_____

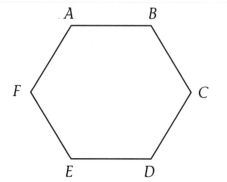

Morning Jumpstarts: Math, Grade 6 © 2013 by Scholastic Teaching Resources

Name _____   Date _____

Number Place

What inequality is shown? Use *m* as the variable.

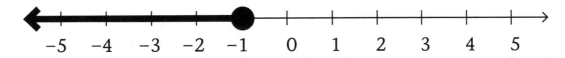

_____

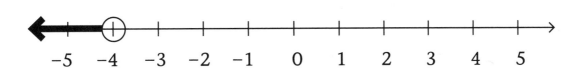

_____

FAST Math

Evaluate each expression for *n* = 4.

$3 + n$ _____ $5.5n$ _____ $7 - n$ _____

$2n + 6$ _____ $\frac{n}{4}$ _____ $n^2 - 5$ _____

$n^2 + n + 7.5$ _____ $3n - 8$ _____ $15 - 2.5n$ _____

Think Tank

Seda cycled 142.5 miles in *y* days. She cycled the same distance each day. Write an expression for the distance she cycled each day.

_____

Show your work in the tank.

Data Place

Four friends joined a track team. The table shows their weights when they began the season and when they finished it.

Display the data in a horizontal double bar graph. Choose numbers for the axis and add all of the labels. Make a key. Give your graph a title.

Person	Start Weight	End Weight
Kiley	110	103
Marcus	104	101
Amir	126	117.5
Toni	84.5	80

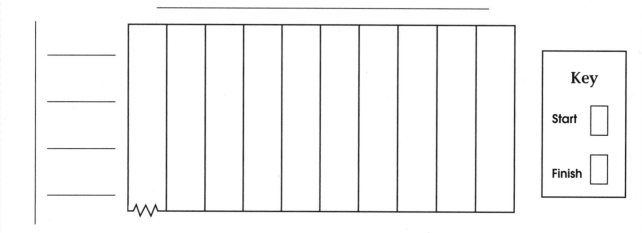

Key

Start ☐

Finish ☐

1. How can you tell who lost the most weight? _____

2. How can you tell who lost the greatest fraction of his or her starting weight?

_____

Puzzler

Fill in the eight squares with the numbers 1–8 so that no two consecutive numbers are connected by a line segment. Use each number once only.

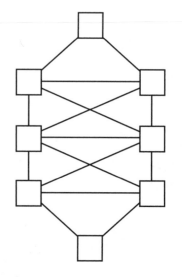

Morning Jumpstarts: Math, Grade 6 © 2013 by Scholastic Teaching Resources

Name _____ Date _____

Number Place

Write each fraction or mixed number as a decimal, and each decimal as a fraction or mixed number.

$\frac{9}{10}$ _____   0.06 _____

0.010 _____ $\frac{5}{100}$ _____

$1\frac{3}{1,000}$ _____   −4.01 _____

−0.014 _____   2.0003 _____

FAST Math

Evaluate each expression for $a = 0.75$ and $b = 2.06$.

$a + b + 8$ _____ $2(a + b)$ _____

$a + b - 2.2$ _____ $3a + 2b$ _____

$a + 4.55 - b$ _____ $(2a + b) \div 4$ _____

Think Tank

These clubs meet after school and on weekends. The glee club meets every third day. The chess club meets every fourth day. The photography club meets every sixth day. All three clubs met today, Thursday. On what day of the week will all three clubs again meet on the same day?

_____

Show your work in the tank.

Data Place

The map shows the
four time zones
in the U.S.A.

**Use the map to answer
the questions.**

U.S. Time Zones

1. If it is 4:30 P.M. in Denver, what time is it in

   Seattle? _____ Dallas? _____ Miami? _____

2. If it is 7:00 A.M. in Boston, what time is it in

   Los Angeles? _____ Dallas? _____ Denver? _____

3. If it is 8:15 P.M. in Miami, what time is it in

   Boston? _____ Seattle? _____ Des Moines? _____

Puzzler

1. Reposition 2 toothpicks to make 7 squares.

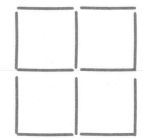

2. Use 10 toothpicks to form 2 squares.

Name _____ Date _____

Number Place

Order the integers from *least* to *greatest*.

−6   −2   −9   −5   _____

−4   4   40   −40   _____

Order the integers from *greatest* to *least*.

−9   −91   19   9   _____

−17   7   −77   17   _____

FAST Math ➔

Simplify each expression.

$7n − 2n$ _____ $n + 2n$ _____

$5n − 2n + 4n$ _____ $5n + 2n − 3s$ _____

$6y + (3y + 2)$ _____ $3(2t + 2t)$ _____

💡 Think Tank

A set of golf clubs and a golf bag together cost $300. Golf balls cost $25 for a dozen. The clubs cost 4 times as much as the bag does. What does the bag cost?

_____

Show your work in the tank.

Data Place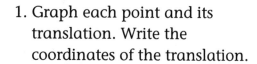

Use the coordinate grid to graph the transformations below.

1. Graph each point and its translation. Write the coordinates of the translation.

   A (5, 4) left 2 units, up 3 units

   _____

   B (−3, 1) right 6 units, down 4 units

   _____

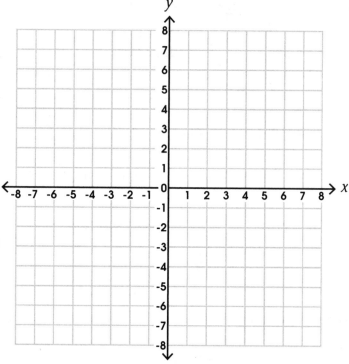

2. Graph triangle *EFG* and its image *E'F'G'*. Write whether the image is a reflection or a translation. Describe the transformation.

   Figure: *E* (−3, 0), F(0, 3), G(3, 0)   Image: *E'* (−2, −2), F'(1, 1), G'(4, −2)

   _____

   _____

Puzzler

Sylvia earns $9.60 an hour at her job. The clocks show when she punched in and when she punched out one afternoon. How much did she earn during that period of time?

_____

68

Name _____ Date _____

Number Place

Rename each pair of fractions using the LCD as their denominator.

$\frac{3}{5}$ and $\frac{1}{4}$ $\frac{9}{10}$ and $\frac{2}{5}$ $\frac{7}{12}$ and $\frac{9}{15}$

_____   _____   _____

Compare. Write <, =, or >.

$\frac{7}{8}$ ____ $\frac{9}{10}$ $\frac{5}{12}$ ____ $\frac{5}{9}$ $\frac{11}{21}$ ____ $\frac{33}{63}$

FAST Math

Write an equation for each statement.

A number w increased by 2.5 is equal to 3.8. _____

The difference between a number y and 82 is 47. _____

A number n divided by 0.5 is equal to 2. _____

The product of a number k and $\frac{3}{8}$ is $1\frac{7}{8}$. _____

💡 Think Tank

Carlos took a 3-day car trip. On the second day he drove 360 miles. On the third day he drove 3 times as far as he did on the first day. If his trip was 1,080 miles long, how far did Carlos drive on the first day?

_____

Show your work in the tank.

Data Place

The line plot shows heights, in stories, of buildings in Deb's town.

Use the data to answer the questions.

Building Heights

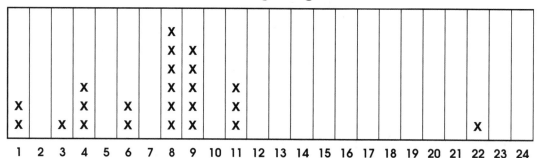

Number of Stories

1. How many buildings are listed in the plot? _____

2. What is the range of the data? _____

3. What is the mode of the data? _____

4. Where are the gaps in the data? _____

5. Which building height is an outlier? _____

Puzzler

In each shape, cross out the fraction or mixed number that does *not* belong.
Then, write one of your own that *does* belong on the line beneath the shape.

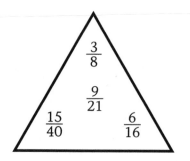

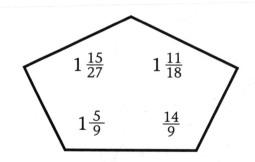

1. _____

2. _____

Name _____ Date _____

Number Place

Order the fractions from *least* to *greatest*.

$\frac{5}{6}$ $\frac{5}{8}$ $\frac{7}{8}$ $\frac{6}{7}$ _____

$\frac{3}{5}$ $\frac{3}{8}$ $\frac{3}{10}$ $\frac{1}{2}$ _____

Order the numbers from *greatest* to *least*.

$\frac{7}{10}$ $\frac{10}{7}$ $1\frac{1}{7}$ 1 _____

$2\frac{2}{3}$ $2\frac{2}{5}$ $2\frac{3}{4}$ $2\frac{1}{2}$ _____

FAST Math ➤

Solve.

$n + 119 = 254$ $n =$ _____ $m + 11 + 17 = 44$ $m =$ _____

$23 + 76 = b$ $b =$ _____ $0 + y = 13$ $y =$ _____

$56 - t = 42$ $t =$ _____ $316 + n = 401 + 226$ $n =$ _____

💡 Think Tank

In its 5-day life, a bug ate 150 smaller bugs. Each day it ate 8 more bugs than it did the day before. How many bugs did it eat on the first day of its life?

_____

Show your work in the tank.

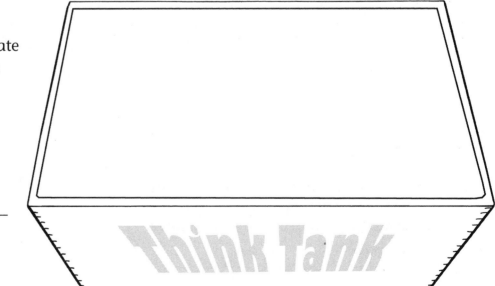

Data Place

The pictograph shows average home attendance at five ballparks.

Use the graph to answer the questions.

Average Home Game Attendance

Fanning Stadium	⚾ ⚾ ⚾ ◗
Fuller Field	⚾ ⚾ ⚾ ⚾ ⚾ ⚾ ◗
Clark Park	⚾ ⚾ ⚾ ⚾ ◗
M-T Stadium	⚾ ⚾ ◗
Wynn Field	⚾ ⚾ ⚾ ⚾ ⚾ ⚾ ⚾ ⚾
Key	⚾ = 6,000 fans

1. Which stadium had the greatest average home attendance? What was it?

   _____

2. Which stadium's average home attendance was 21,000 less than that of

   Wynn Field? _____

3. The average home attendance at Fanning Stadium was about two-fifths of that

   of which stadium? _____

4. Which stadium's average home attendance was closest to the mean of the data?

   _____

5. What is the mean absolute deviation of the attendance data? _____

Puzzler

This square is divided into four congruent rectangles.
Each rectangle has a perimeter of 20 units.
What is the perimeter and area of the square?

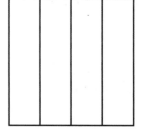

_____

Name _____ Date _____

Number Place

Compare. Write **<**, **=**, or **>**.

2.005 _____ $2\frac{5}{100}$ 1.25 _____ $1\frac{1}{4}$

3.7 _____ $3\frac{1}{7}$ 22.6 _____ $2\frac{2}{6}$

4.20 _____ four and two hundredths

six and fifty thousandths _____ $6\frac{5}{100}$

FAST Math ➔

Solve.

$38n = 760$ $n =$ _____ $17w = 255$ $w =$ _____

$y \div 75 = 184$ $y =$ _____ $\frac{s}{15} = 120$ $s =$ _____

$200 = 80m$ $m =$ _____ $650 = p \div 13$ $p =$ _____

💡 Think Tank

You know the price of a week's pass to a gym. You also know the price of a yearly membership. How can you determine how much you would save in a year by buying the yearly membership rather than paying for one week at a time?

_____

_____

_____

_____

Show your work in the tank.

Data Place

The table shows scoring
in a football league.

Touchdown	6 points
Touchdown With Extra Point	7 points
Field Goal	3 points
Safety.	2 points

The Modem played the Drive.

**Use the clues to fill in the scoreboard.
Then answer the question.**

• At the end of the first quarter, the score was 10–7.

• At the end of the second quarter, the score was 15–16.

• At the end of the third quarter, the score was 32–29.

• At the end of the fourth quarter, the score was 41–43.

• The Modem had a field goal in each quarter, but only one safety in the game. It was in the second quarter.

• The Drive had at least 1 touchdown with extra point in each quarter.

Quarter	1	2	3	4	Final Score
Modem					
Drive					

Who won the game? _____

Puzzler

Show how you would use line segments to divide this figure into
two figures having the same size and shape.

Morning Jumpstarts: Math, Grade 6 © 2013 by Scholastic Teaching Resources

Name _____ Date _____

Number Place

Compare. Write **<**, **=**, or **>**.

$\dfrac{5}{8}$ ____ $\dfrac{7}{10}$ $-\dfrac{5}{6}$ ____ -5 $\dfrac{1}{2}$ ____ $-\dfrac{1}{2}$

$\dfrac{3}{4}$ ____ 0.8 $-\dfrac{2}{3}$ ____ 0 $-2\dfrac{1}{3}$ ____ -3

FAST Math →

Solve.

$n + 1.5 = 2.7$ $n = $ _____ $m - 11.6 = 14.4$ $m = $ _____

$2.3 + 0.06 = b$ $b = $ _____ $\dfrac{y}{2.5} = 20$ $y = $ _____

$5.6t = 19.04$ $t = $ _____ $1.13 = r \div 0.09$ $r = $ _____

💡 Think Tank

Pau's pool has an area of 615 square feet. It is $20\dfrac{1}{2}$ feet wide and $5\dfrac{1}{2}$ feet deep. The pool is rectangular. How much water will it hold if filled to the top?

_____

Show your work in the tank.

Data Place

The two graphs show dog-training DVD sales.

Use the data to answer the questions.

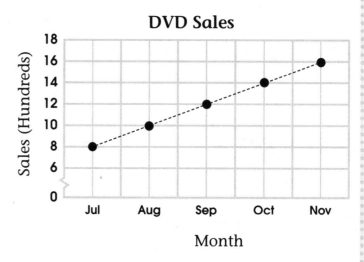

1. Do both graphs show the same data? _____

2. How do the graphs give a different impression of the data? _____

_____

3. Which graph gives the impression that
   sales are increasing more dramatically? _____

Puzzler

Here is a way to name 4. It uses fraction bars, a plus sign,
and the digits 1, 2, 3, 4, and 8 *once* each:

$$3\frac{1}{2} + \frac{4}{8} = 4$$

Now you try. Use fraction bars, a plus sign,
and the digits 1, 3, 4, 5, 6, and 8 *once* each to name 9.

Name _____ Date _____

Number Place

Order the numbers from *least* to *greatest*.

1.6	1.2	−1.2	−1.6	_____
$\frac{1}{2}$	$-\frac{1}{2}$	$-1\frac{1}{2}$	1	_____
10.1	−10.01	−10	10	_____
$2\frac{1}{4}$	−2	$-2\frac{1}{4}$	2	_____

FAST Math ▶

Solve.

$n + 1\frac{3}{5} = 3\frac{3}{10}$ $n =$ _____

$b - \frac{4}{7} = \frac{5}{14}$ $b =$ _____

$t - \frac{3}{5} = \frac{4}{5}$ $t =$ _____

$\frac{7}{9} - m = \frac{2}{9}$ $m =$ _____

$y = 2\frac{1}{4} + 5\frac{1}{8}$ $y =$ _____

$\frac{5}{8} + k = 3\frac{1}{8}$ $k =$ _____

💡 Think Tank

Dina stacks 220 cans of soup at the store where she works. The top layer has 1 can. The next layer has 3 cans, the next has 6, then 10, and so on. How many layers are there?

_____

How many cans are in the bottom layer?

_____

Show your work in the tank.

Data Place

The stem-and-leaf plot shows the age at inauguration of 15 American presidents first inaugurated between 1923 and 2009.

Use the data to answer the questions below.

1. How many presidents were in their forties when they were inaugurated?

    _____

Age of 15 American Presidents at First Inauguration (1923–2009)	
Stem	Leaf
4	3 6 7
5	1 1 2 4 4 5 6
6	0 1 2 4 9

2. How many were 54 when inaugurated? _____

3. How old was the oldest of these presidents at inauguration? _____

4. What is the range of the ages of these presidents

    at their inaugurations? _____

5. What is the median age of these presidents at their inaugurations? _____

6. How many presidents were at least 55 when they were inaugurated? _____

Puzzler

Daniel is placing the DVDs he owns on a shelf. He has between 40 and 50 DVDs. He wants to place the same number on each shelf. If he uses 4 shelves, there are 3 left over. If he uses 6 shelves, 5 are left over.

How many DVDs does Daniel have? _____

Name _____ Date _____

Number Place

Circle the numbers divisible by 5.

400   7,512   85   1,101   145,405

Circle the numbers divisible by 4.

234   92   164   9,462   65,408

Circle the numbers divisible by 6.

330   573   132   1,172   12,408

FAST Math ➤

Solve.

$\frac{5}{8}n = 95$ $n =$ _____

$5b = 5\frac{5}{8}$ $b =$ _____

$\frac{8}{15}t = 1\frac{1}{9}$ $t =$ _____

$\frac{5}{8}m \div \frac{8}{9} = 21$ $m =$ _____

$w \div \frac{2}{3} = \frac{6}{7}$ $w =$ _____

$2p + \frac{1}{2}p = 25$ $p =$ _____

💡 Think Tank

Six friends finish two-thirds of a job in one day. They share the work equally. What fraction of the day's work does each do?

_____

Show your work in the tank.

Data Place

Place the numbers 1, 2, 3, 6, 7, 8, 11, and 14 where they belong in the diagram.

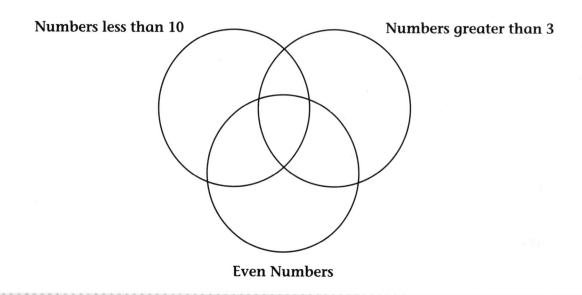

Numbers less than 10   Numbers greater than 3

Even Numbers

Puzzler

The map shows where dinosaur bones have been found. The four paleontologists on the site want to divide the region so that each can examine the same number of bones. Show how this can be accomplished using only two straight lines.

Each • is a location of a bone.

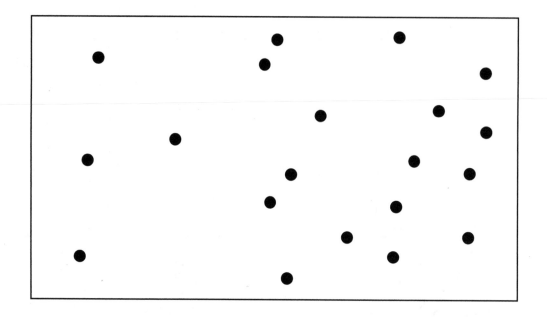

Morning Jumpstarts: Math, Grade 6 © 2013 by Scholastic Teaching Resources

Name _____ Date _____

Number Place

Write whether the number is divisible by 2, 3, 4, 5, 6, 8, 9, and/or 10.

333   8,410   67,704   90,990   352,860

_____ _____ _____ _____ _____

FAST Math →

Add or subtract.

+3 + +2 = _____   +3 + −5 = _____   +6 − +2 = _____

+5 − −5 = _____   +7 − +7 = _____   −7 + −8 = _____

−2 − +2 = _____   −4 + +2 + −6 = _____   +3 + −2 + −5 = _____

Think Tank

Art is making 3 pennants in the shape of isosceles triangles. Each will have a $1\frac{3}{4}$-foot base and will be $5\frac{1}{3}$ feet long. Find the total area of all 3 pennants.

_____

Show your work in the tank.

Data Place

Here are the numbers of points the school's basketball team scored in home games this season.

| 47 54 70 62 59 62 82 66 62 73 55 82 59 |

Make a stem-and-leaf plot for this set of data.
Find the range, median, and mode of the data.

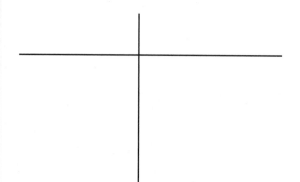

1. Range _____   2. Median _____   3. Mode _____

4. Which measure best represents the data? _____

Puzzler

Choose any integer. Follow the 12 steps to see a number trick.

1. Add −15.   2. Subtract −13.   3. Add +19.

4. Subtract −9.   5. Subtract +4.   6. Subtract +17.

7. Add +8.   8. Subtract −12.   9. Add +11.

10. Subtract +2.   11. Subtract +16.   12. Add −18.

What do you notice? _____

Choose another integer and try the trick again.

82

Name _____ Date _____

Number Place

Is the number prime, composite, or neither? Write *p*, *c*, or *n*.

32 _____   19 _____   81 _____   41 _____   207 _____

Write True or False. Then explain your choice.

All prime numbers are odd numbers. _____

_____

The sum of two prime numbers is a composite number. _____

_____

FAST Math

Find the product.

+4 × +2 = _____   +8 × −5 = _____   +6 × +21 = _____

+50 × −5 = _____   0 × +7 = _____   −12 × −8 = _____

−2 × +20 = _____   −4 × +2 × −6 = _____   +3 × −2 × +7 = _____

Think Tank

The average daily temperature in Calgary for each of seven days was −2°C, −3°C, −1°C, +2°C, −2°C, +4°C and +1°C. What was the median temperature in Calgary that week?

_____

Show your work in the tank.

Data Place

Here are the scores Nora got on her social studies tests in this marking period.

63	90	52	90	56	73	61

Select from mean, median, or mode to answer the following questions. Then give the actual measure.

1. What measure of average should Nora's teacher use to describe her scores

   most accurately? _____

2. What measure should Nora use to show her scores in the best light?

   _____

3. What measure would describe Nora's scores the least favorably? _____

   _____

Puzzler

Write *Yes* or *No* to answer each question. If *No*, explain why.

1. Can you make a triangle that has

   two obtuse angles? _____

2. Can you make a quadrilateral that has

   no right angles? _____

3. Can you make a pentagon that has

   four obtuse angles? _____

4. Can you make a parallelogram that has

   four congruent acute angles? _____

Name _____ Date _____

Number Place

Write the absolute value of each number.

−326 _____   −15 _____   18 _____   −4.5 _____ $-\frac{2}{5}$ _____

−0.6 _____   −22 _____   0 _____   −87 _____ $-\frac{5}{8}$ _____

FAST Math

Add or subtract. Write your answer in simplest form.

$+3\frac{1}{2} + {+2} =$ _____ $+2 + {-\frac{5}{8}} =$ _____ $+6 - {+\frac{2}{3}} =$ _____

$+\frac{5}{8} - {-\frac{5}{8}} =$ _____ $+\frac{7}{20} - {+\frac{7}{20}} =$ _____ $-0.5 + {-8.5} =$ _____

$$\begin{array}{r} -2.2 \\ -\ +2.5 \\ \hline \end{array}$$
$$\begin{array}{r} -\frac{4}{5} \\ +\ +\frac{2}{5} \\ \hline \end{array}$$
$$\begin{array}{r} +\frac{3}{4} \\ +\ -\frac{2}{3} \\ \hline \end{array}$$

Think Tank

Five painters can paint 5 houses in 5 days. How many days will it take 2 painters to paint 1 house?

_____

Show your work in the tank.

Data Place

Complete the function table for the function $y = x + 0.5$.

Then draw the graph of the function on the coordinate grid.

x	x + 0.5	(x, y)
0		
1		
2		

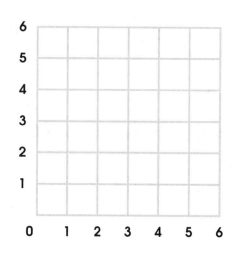

Is $y = x + 0.5$ a linear function? _____

How do you know? _____

Puzzler

Each clock is a mirror reflection.

Tell the actual time for each.

_____   _____   _____

Name _____ Date _____

Number Place

Express each using exponents. Then write the product.

$2 \times 2 \times 2$ _____ $2 \times 2 \times 3 \times 3 \times 3$ _____

$3 \times 3 \times 3 \times 3 \times 4$ _____ $5 \times 12 \times 5 \times 5$ _____

$3 \times 3 \times 4 \times 4 \times 4$ _____ $6 \times 2 \times 6 \times 2$ _____

FAST Math

Replace the variable with an integer to make the inequality true.

$n > 9$ _____ $m < -21$ _____

$b < -5$ _____ $y \leq -1$ _____

$n + 3 > 5$ _____ $r + 2 \leq -2$ _____

💡 Think Tank

A baseball game being played in Seattle is televised in Baltimore, where Wanda is watching it. The game began at 8:05 P.M. in Seattle and lasted for $2\frac{3}{4}$ hours. Wanda turned off the game as soon as it ended. What time did she turn off the television?

_____

Show your work in the tank.

Data Place

The scatter plot shows temperatures one evening.

Use the data to answer the questions.

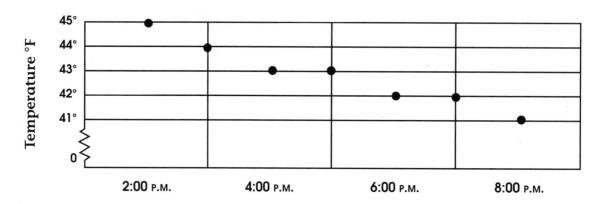

1. What correlation, if any, is there between temperature and time? Explain.

_____

2. Over what period of time was the temperature at or below 43°F? _____

Puzzler

Phan's property is in the shape of a square, with 100 meters on a side. His neighbor has a hungry goat so Phan wants to fence in the property. The fence will have a post every 10 meters. How many posts will the fence have?

_____

Draw a sketch to help you figure it out.

Morning Jumpstarts: Math, Grade 6 © 2013 by Scholastic Teaching Resources

Name _____ Date _____

Number Place

Compare. Write **<**, **=**, or **>**.

2^3 ___ 3^2 2^5 ___ 2×5 4^3 ___ 64

5^3 ___ 2^6 3^4 ___ $2^3 \times 3^2$ 6^3 ___ $2 \times 5 \times 5 \times 5$

2^2 ___ $(0.2)^2$ $(\frac{1}{2})^3$ ___ $(\frac{1}{4})^3$ $(0.6)^3$ ___ $(\frac{1}{2})^2$

FAST Math

Write each ratio in simplest form.

4 to 12   8 : 20 $\dfrac{21}{63}$ 12 to 18   50 : 30

_____   _____   _____   _____   _____

24 to 12   14 : 3.5 $\dfrac{12}{84}$ 1.2 to 2.0   5 : 2.5

_____   _____   _____   _____   _____

Think Tank

What is the ratio
of infielders to outfielders?

_____

What is the ratio
of infielders to players?

_____

Show your work
in the tank.

Players on a Baseball Team

3 outfielders

4 infielders

1 catcher

1 pitcher

Think Tank

Data Place

This quilt is made of 25 square sections sewn together. The quilt represents one whole.

What percent is represented by

1. the dotted sections? _____

2. the starred sections? _____

3. the dotted, starred, and circle sections?

    _____

4. all the sections? _____

5. all but the sections with crossed lines? _____

6. 1 quilt plus all the dotted and circle sections? _____

Puzzler

Make one straight cut in this figure so that the two pieces you form can be reassembled into a square.
Draw a dotted line to show where to cut.

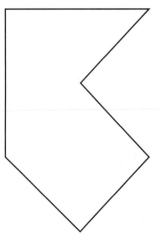

90

Name _____ Date _____

Number Place

Find the prime factorization. Write it in exponential form.

8 _____   32 _____   125 _____

50 _____   60 _____   96 _____

FAST Math ▸

Circle each ratio equivalent to the first ratio.

3 : 2	30 to 2	9 to 6	$\frac{15}{9}$	36 : 24
$\frac{10}{7}$	20 : 14	25 to 14	1 to 0.7	$\frac{1}{7}$
45 to 25	50 : 30	9 to 5	5 to 9	$\frac{40}{20}$

Which ratios are equivalent? Write = or ≠.

$\frac{7}{8}$ ___ 16 to 14 $\frac{5}{12}$ ___ 15 : 36   10 : 4 ___ $\frac{25}{10}$

$\frac{2}{5}$ ___ 10 to 4 $\frac{36}{48}$ ___ 3 : 4   1.5 : 0.5 ___ $\frac{3}{1}$

💡 Think Tank

Becca plays on a basketball team. She has 3 uniform tops, 2 pairs of shorts, and 2 pairs of sneakers. How many different outfits can she put together if she always wears a top, shorts, and sneakers when she plays?

_____

Show your work in the tank.

Morning Jumpstarts: Math, Grade 6 © 2013 by Scholastic Teaching Resources

Data Place

Fiona opens a grocery in a town that already has two. She wants to offer the lowest prices. To do this, she figures out which of her competitors has the lowest unit prices for what she sells. She then make her unit price 2¢ less. But, Fiona sells her products only in packages of 5!

Complete the table to find Fiona's price for five of the items shown.

Item	Gil's Grocery	Mira's Market	Fiona's Foods
Corn Muffin	4 for $6	10 for $18	5 for
Yogurt	4 for $3.40	6 for $4.62	5 for
Canned Tuna	6 for $7.50	4 for $4.88	5 for

Puzzler

For each object, draw the *top* view, *front* view, and *side* view.

Object	Top View	Front View	Side View

Name _____ Date _____

Number Place

Write two equivalent fractions or mixed numbers for each.

$\frac{1}{2}$ _____ $\frac{3}{5}$ _____ $-\frac{3}{8}$ _____

$1\frac{1}{2}$ _____ $-3\frac{2}{5}$ _____ $5\frac{3}{10}$ _____

$-\frac{1}{4}$ _____ $-\frac{2}{7}$ _____ $-3\frac{7}{8}$ _____

FAST Math

Find the unit rate or unit price.

28 miles in 4 hours _____   6 DVDs for $42 _____

96 feet in 12 seconds _____   6 cards for $21 _____

24 pages read in 16 minutes _____   1 dozen cans for $7.20 _____

Think Tank

A bottle has a capacity of 1.8 L. Two-thirds of it holds eye care solution. If each dose is 2 mL, how many doses are in the bottle?

_____

Show your work in the tank.

Data Place

Here are won-lost records of the top five pitchers in Big Mesa Little League history. Remarkably, all these stars had the same ratio of wins to losses.

Complete the table. Then answer the question.

Player	Years	Won	Lost
Lefty Lebowitz	1988–1990	42	14
Hands Hansen	1997–1999		16
Stringbean Gomez	2004–2006	36	
Baby Face Jonas	2008–2010		11
Big Mo Tanaka	2012–	15	

Legendary great Ted "Kid" Toomer won 57 games in the 1970s. What is the greatest number of games Kid could have lost and still have had a better record than any pitcher in the table? _____

Puzzler

A dot cube has these faces:

Draw the face opposite.

Draw the face opposite.

94

Name _____   Date _____

Number Place

Rename in simplest form.

$\frac{12}{24}$ ____ $\frac{16}{20}$ ____ $\frac{3}{18}$ ____ $-\frac{16}{28}$ ____ $-\frac{20}{32}$ ____

$-\frac{6}{27}$ ____ $-\frac{9}{45}$ ____ $1\frac{6}{8}$ ____ $1\frac{6}{15}$ ____ $-2\frac{14}{18}$ ____

FAST Math ▶

Do the ratios form a proportion? Write yes or no.

$\frac{2}{3} \overset{?}{=} \frac{6}{9}$ ____ $\frac{2}{5} \overset{?}{=} \frac{6}{20}$ ____ $\frac{7}{2} \overset{?}{=} \frac{14}{5}$ ____

$\frac{2}{7} \overset{?}{=} \frac{6}{24}$ ____ $\frac{2}{8} \overset{?}{=} \frac{8}{32}$ ____ $\frac{1}{3} \overset{?}{=} \frac{6}{18}$ ____

$\frac{12}{30} \overset{?}{=} \frac{6}{60}$ ____ $\frac{8}{3} \overset{?}{=} \frac{40}{9}$ ____ $\frac{81}{3} \overset{?}{=} \frac{27}{1}$ ____

💡 Think Tank

A rectangular rug measures 35 feet by 28 feet. How many feet must be cut from both its length and width so that the ratio of the shorter side to the longer side is 3 to 4?

_____

Show your work in the tank.

Data Place

Seven cards have geometric figures on them.
What could each ratio represent?

1. $\frac{1}{2}$ _____

2. $\frac{2}{7}$ _____

3. $\frac{1}{6}$ _____

4. $\frac{3}{1}$ _____

5. $\frac{2}{3}$ _____

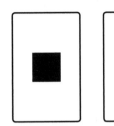

Puzzler

Draw three squares to separate each ✪ from every other ✪.

Hint: Think "inside the box."

✪   ✪   ✪

✪   ✪   ✪

✪   ✪   ✪

Morning Jumpstarts: Math, Grade 6 © 2013 by Scholastic Teaching Resources

Name _____ Date _____

Number Place

Express each fraction as a mixed number in simplest form.

$\frac{12}{7}$ ____ $\frac{16}{6}$ ____ $-\frac{32}{12}$ ____ $\frac{36}{8}$ ____ $-\frac{20}{12}$ ____

Express each mixed number as a fraction in simplest form.

$-1\frac{2}{8}$ ____ $3\frac{7}{20}$ ____ $2\frac{8}{18}$ ____ $6\frac{5}{15}$ ____ $-2\frac{9}{39}$ ____

FAST Math

Find the value of *n* in each proportion.

$\frac{2}{5} = \frac{6}{n}$ _____ $\frac{n}{7} = \frac{6}{14}$ _____ $\frac{1}{n} = \frac{4}{52}$ _____

$\frac{n}{8} = \frac{6}{24}$ _____ $\frac{8}{5} = \frac{n}{35}$ _____ $\frac{5}{3} = \frac{n}{18}$ _____

$\frac{12}{20} = \frac{n}{60}$ _____ $\frac{n}{3} = \frac{42}{9}$ _____ $\frac{72}{9} = \frac{24}{n}$ _____

Think Tank

A cube has the same volume in cubic inches as its surface area in square inches. What is the length of one of the edges of the cube?

_____

Show your work in the tank.

Data Place

Wilson has a part-time job. The double line graph shows his monthly income and expenses for 6 months.

Use the data to answer the questions.

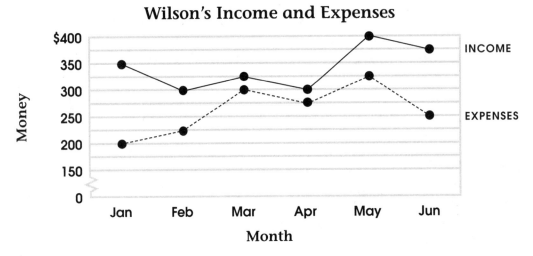

Wilson's Income and Expenses

1. What was the difference between Wilson's income and expenses in May? _____

2. In which month did Wilson save the most money? _____

3. To the nearest dollar, what was the mean monthly difference between Wilson's income and his expenses? _____

4. In which month were Wilson's expenses the greatest percent of his income?

   _____

Puzzler

For each object, draw the *top* view, *front* view, and *side* view.

Object	Top View	Front View	Side View

Morning Jumpstarts: Math, Grade 6 © 2013 by Scholastic Teaching Resources

Name _____ Date _____

Number Place

Write each fraction as a decimal. Write each decimal as a fraction or mixed number in simplest form.

$-\dfrac{7}{10}$ _____ -0.06 _____

0.040 _____ $-\dfrac{3}{100}$ _____

$-7\dfrac{4}{5}$ _____ -44.55 _____

-0.014 _____ $61\dfrac{1}{8}$ _____

FAST Math

Write each percent as a fraction or mixed number in simplest form.

70% _____   5% _____   64% _____   150% _____

95% _____   225% _____   12% _____   124% _____

Write each fraction as a percent.

$\dfrac{2}{5}$ _____ $\dfrac{7}{8}$ _____ $\dfrac{24}{30}$ _____ $\dfrac{5}{8}$ _____

$\dfrac{8}{5}$ _____ $\dfrac{1}{25}$ _____ $\dfrac{7}{100}$ _____ $\dfrac{5}{4}$ _____

Think Tank

Two trapezoids are similar. The longer bases are 12 cm and 18 cm. If the length of the shorter base of the smaller trapezoid is 4 cm, how long is the shorter base of the larger trapezoid?

_____

Show your work in the tank.

Data Place

The circle graph shows the favorite kinds of TV programs the kids in Ms. Couch's class watch.

Use the data to answer the questions.

What percent of the students chose the following?

1. comedy _____

2. game show _____

3. sports or reality _____

4. drama or talk show _____

What percent did not choose the following?

5. comedy or sports _____

6. game show or drama _____

Favorite Kinds of TV Shows

Puzzler

Make a sketch to help you solve this problem.

Coach Koch arranges her basketball team in a circle. Her 12 players are evenly spaced around it. Each player passes the ball to the player directly opposite. The players are wearing uniforms numbered 1–12, and are standing in number order.
Who passes the ball to player 7?

_____

Morning Jumpstarts: Math, Grade 6 © 2013 by Scholastic Teaching Resources

Name _____ Date _____

Number Place

Write each phrase as an algebraic expression.

one less than *r* _____

n divided by 7 _____

One fourth of y _____

k increased by *m* _____

the ratio of *w* and 8 _____

the product of 5 and *t* _____

You walk a mile in *x* minutes. How many miles in 60 minutes? _____

FAST Math

Write each percent as a decimal.

40% _____   8% _____   1% _____   11.5% _____

216% _____   0.7% _____   0.3% _____   125% _____

Write each decimal as a percent.

0.2 _____   0.02 _____   0.875 _____   3.5 _____

1.8 _____   0.07 _____   1.25 _____   0.995 _____

Think Tank

A 24-foot flagpole casts a 36-foot shadow. At the same time, Luisa casts a 90-inch shadow. How tall is Luisa?

_____

Show your work in the tank.

Data Place

Box-and-whisker plots show how data is distributed.
This one shows golf scores.

Use the box-and-whisker plot to answer the questions.

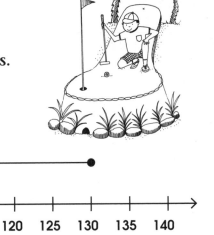

70   75   80   85   90   95   100   105   110   115   120   125   130   135   140

1. What is the upper extreme of the data? _____

2. What is the lowest score any golfer got? _____

3. What is the median of the data? _____

4. What is the median of the upper quartile? _____

5. What is the median of the lower quartile? _____

Puzzler

What percent of the figure is shaded? _____

Name _____ Date _____

Number Place

Write the opposite of each.

−6 _____   8.5 _____   −3 $\frac{1}{2}$ _____   −0.04 _____

−12 _____   4 $\frac{1}{4}$ _____   −3.5 _____   −1.007 _____

32 _____   53 _____   −3.05 _____   −$\frac{3}{8}$ _____

FAST Math

Find the percent of the number. Use mental math when you can.

20% of 50 _____   15% of 60 _____   50% of 40 _____

12.5% of 64 _____   25% of 8 _____   16 $\frac{2}{3}$ % of 30 _____

Compare. Write **<**, **=**, or **>**.

20% of 20 ____ 25% of 16   62.5% of 40 ____ 83 $\frac{1}{3}$ % of 24

Think Tank

Forty-eight of the 60 members of a chorus sang in the performance. What percent of the chorus did not sing?

_____

Show your work in the tank.

Data Place

When you spin the two spinners together, 12 outcomes are possible.

Use the spinners to answer the questions.

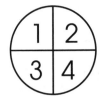 

1. Are all 12 outcomes equally likely? _____

2. You spin the spinner at the left. What is the probability that you will spin an even number? _____

3. You spin the spinner at the right. What is the probability that you will spin a number less than 5? _____

You spin both spinners. What is the probability that the following will occur?

4. A 2 and a 5 _____

5. At least one 3 _____

6. Two numbers with a sum of 5 _____

7. Two numbers with a sum of 7 _____

Puzzler

Write *True* or *False*.

1. Any number on a number line is greater than any number to its left. _____

2. The number −6 is to the left of −9 on the number line. _____

3. If *x* is a positive integer, then *x* > than 0. _____

4. Any positive integer has a greater absolute value than any negative integer. _____

Name _____ Date _____

Number Place

Name the property shown. Write *commutative, associative, identity, or distributive.*

$4 + 7 = 7 + 4$ _____

$(3 + 8) + 6 = 3 + (8 + 6)$ _____

$8 \times 1 = 8$ _____

$-17 + 0 = -17$ _____

$3 \times (8 + 7) = (3 \times 8) + (3 \times 7)$ _____

FAST Math ➤

Find the percent.

What % of 5 is 3? _____   6 is what % of 12? _____

60 is what % of 240? _____   What % of 25 is 20? _____

4.6 is what % of 50? _____   What % of 50 is 125? _____

💡 Think Tank

On a typical day at Curie Middle School 4.5% of the 600 students are absent. How many absences are there in a typical 5-day school week?

_____

Show your work in the tank.

Morning Jumpstarts: Math, Grade 6 © 2013 by Scholastic Teaching Resources

Data Place

Use the figure to answer the questions.

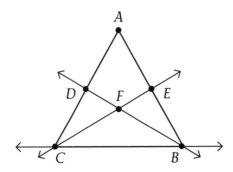

1. Name two lines passing through *F.* _____

2. Name four rays with endpoints at *F.* _____

3. Name three angles with a vertex at *B.* _____

4. Name three angles with a vertex at *D.* _____

5. Name a quadrilateral. _____

6. Name an obtuse triangle. _____

Puzzler

Meg is on one side of a river with her brother, her sister, and a cake. She has to row the kids and the cake across the river. But there's room to take only one thing with her in her small boat. The problem is that she can't leave her brother alone with her sister, nor her sister alone with the cake. Explain how Meg can get everything safely across.

_____

_____

_____

_____

Morning Jumpstarts: Math, Grade 6 © 2013 by Scholastic Teaching Resources

Name _____   Date _____

Number Place

Read the newspaper headlines. Circle the ones that you think
have rounded numbers.

- *POPULATION OF BOLIVIA RISES TO 10,000,000*

- *250,000 AT OUTDOOR MUSIC FESTIVAL*

- *32,550 ATTEND STATE FAIR*

- *BANK LOSES $2.45 MILLION IN 3RD QUARTER*

- *CYCLIST CROSSES NATION IN 380 HOURS*

FAST Math ▶

Find the original number.

50% of *n* is 45 _____   12 is $16\frac{2}{3}$ % of *n* _____

$12\frac{1}{2}$ % of *n* is 48 _____   18 is 40% of *n* _____

550 is 22% of *n* _____   19% of *n* is 152 _____

💡 Think Tank

Noah tosses a 1–6 number
cube. What is the probability
that he will toss a number
greater than 2?

_____

What is the probability
that he will toss a 7?

_____

**Show your work
in the tank.**

JUMPSTART 50

Side B

Data Place

You can use more than one type of graph to show the same data. The best graph to use depends upon what it is about the data that you want to show.

Write *bar*, *line*, *circle*, or *histogram* to show what type of graph would be best to show the data described.

1. You want to compare the first month's book sales of two biographies of a famous actor. _____

2. You want to show how your cat spends a typical 24-hour day. _____

3. A rock group just released a new CD. You want to show monthly sales over a 6-month time period. _____

4. You want to show what music people like in their teens, twenties, thirties, and forties. _____

Puzzler

Ross has 6 silver coins that look and feel exactly alike. But one is a fake, and weighs less than the others. Ross has a balance scale. How can he identify the fake coin using only two weighings on the scale?

_____

_____

_____

_____

Morning Jumpstarts: Math, Grade 6 © 2013 by Scholastic Teaching Resources

Answers

Jumpstart 1

Number Place: (Left to right) 1,352,350; 6,802,387; 2,308,122,050; 19,663,000,000; 7,500,000; 1,005,554,799,000; 499,020,000; 6,999,500,000

Fast Math: 19; 11; 51; 42

Think Tank: 35

Data Place:

Music Group	Tally	Number
Loud Enough	ㅐㅐ ㅐㅐ II	12
Bunny and Hare	ㅐㅐ III	8
The Bugs	ㅐㅐ ㅐㅐ ㅐㅐ ㅐㅐ	20
Squash	ㅐㅐ ㅐㅐ ㅐㅐ I	16

Puzzler: Answers may vary; sample answer: 358 + 469 + 172

Jumpstart 2

Number Place: hundred million; million; ten million; ten billion; billion; hundred million

Fast Math: Answers may vary; sample answers: 9,432 + 657; 7,956 – 423

Think Tank: 4,400 ft²

Data Place: 1. Anchorage **2.** Seattle **3.** Boston

Puzzler: HOSPITAL; POLICE STATION; RAMP CLOSED

Jumpstart 3

Number Place: 300,000,000,010; 59,000,000,130; 606,000,000,000; 32,000,000,000,104

Fast Math: (Left to right) 360; 30,000; 280,000; 49,000; 8,000; 900,000; 48,000; 30,000; 2,800,000; 500,000; 500,000; 10,000

Think Tank: 6 hens

Data Place: 1. ¼ **2.** ⅜ **3.** fantasy and mystery **4.** 18; 17

Puzzler:

387	**400**	383	391	408
393	405	**389**	397	**385**
399	382	395	407	386
409	**388**	396	**384**	392
381	**394**	406	390	**398**

Jumpstart 4

Number Place:

Number	Millions	Thousands	Hundreds
1,700,000	1.7	1,700	17,000
8,000,000	8	8,000	80,000
1,800,000,000	1,800	1,800,000	18,000,000
25,000,000,000	25,000	25,000,000	250,000,000
34,500,000	34.5	34,500	345,000

Fast Math: 9,000; 14,100; 38,100; 68,000

Think Tank: 12 mph; 6 mi

Data Place: 1. Basset EX **2.** Toadster **3.** Toadster, Sloth GT **4.** 65,000 **5.** 97,000

Puzzler: 210 blocks

Jumpstart 5

Number Place: (Left to right) 1,000; 1; 10,000,000; 100,000,000; 10,000; 10; 100; 1,000,000

Fast Math: (Left to right) 6,000; 8,000; 25,000; 480,000; 180,000; 600,000

Think Tank: Ike; he has 3 quarters and 4 dimes.

Data Place: 1. 1 h **2.** ¾ h **3.** Wednesday **4.** Thursday; 4¾ h

Puzzler: All answers should be 109,989.

Jumpstart 6

Number Place: (Left to right) 10²; 10⁰; 10⁴; 10⁶; 10³; 10⁷

Fast Math: (Left to right) 80; 40; 800; 90; 120; 50; >; >

Think Tank: tea

Data Place: 1. Apr. 19, 20, 21, 22, and 23 **2.** Apr. 11, 12, and 13 **3.** Apr. 28 and 29 **4.** Apr. 17, 29 **5.** Apr. 15, 17, 19

Puzzler: The difference in digits is 4 in each number.

Jumpstart 7

Number Place: $(1 \times 10^3) + (5 \times 10^0)$; $(2 \times 10^2) + (1 \times 10^1) + (6 \times 10^0)$; $(4 \times 10^4) + (2 \times 10^3) + (9 \times 10^2) + (6 \times 10^0)$; $(8 \times 10^5) + (4 \times 10^4)$; $(2 \times 10^6) + (7 \times 10^4) + (5 \times 10^3)$; $(3 \times 10^9) + (6 \times 10^8) + (6 \times 10^7)$

Fast Math: (Left to right) Answers may vary; sample answers: 400; 700; 900; 50; 90; 8,000; 90,000; 12; 10,000

Think Tank: 93,499,999 mi

Data Place: 1. 1,156 mi **2.** Chicago and Denver **3.** Denver and Cleveland **4.** 1,478 mi **5.** Detroit and Chicago **6.** Omaha and Denver

Puzzler: 12 kg

Jumpstart 8

Number Place: 90,600; 320,700; 5,409,006; 600,010,080

Fast Math: (Left to right) 169 R31; 1,001; 2,153; 108 R14; 443 R63; 172; 3 R433; 503; 312 R74

Think Tank: 6 + 7 + 8 + 9 = 30

Data Place: 1. (4, 1) **2.** (1, 9) **3.** (9, 1) **4.** (2, 5) **5.** H, Computer City **6.** D, Newsstand **7.** E, Audio Mart **8.** G, Bob's Bakery

Puzzler: A = 2; B = 1; C = 7; D = 8

Jumpstart 9

Number Place: <; >; >; =; >; >

Fast Math: 2.2; 100.2; 1.3

Think Tank: 309,649 mi²

Data Place: 1. scalene **2.** isosceles

Puzzler:

Jumpstart 10

Number Place: (Left to right) 0.8; 0.06; 0.63; 0.016; 0.0009; 1.02

Fast Math: (Left to right) 15.56; 1.5633; 2.787; 10.3078; 5.9524; 0.165

Think Tank: Rosie makes money; $500

Data Place: 1. 13 **2.** 55 **3.** 95 **4.** 45, about 89, 95, 95 **5.** 20, about 92, 95, 95

Puzzler: 1. The product of the month's number and the day's number equals the last two digits of the year. **2.** January 12, February 6, and March 4, 2012

Jumpstart 11

Number Place: $y = 0.4$; $w = 0.7$

Fast Math: (Left to right) 8; 63; 10; 80; 20; 40; 90; 60

Think Tank: 39 in; 3,281 ft

Data Place:

Quarter	1	2	3	4	Final Score
Bees	3	6	10	8	27
Moths	3	7	2	14	26

Puzzler: 10

Jumpstart 12

Number Place: 0.00012; 60.09; 0.0047; 7,000.022

Fast Math: (Left to right) 0.2; 0.63; 4; 20; 0.07; 3; 3,024; 504.7

Think Tank: 6.45 oz

Data Place: 21.5 mpg

Puzzler:

Jumpstart 13

Number Place:

Number	Nearest 1,000	Nearest 100,000
389,900	390,000	400,000
1,844,938	1,845,000	1,800,000
24,061,562	24,062,000	24,100,000

Fast Math: 0.0017; 0.6; 2.198; 2,370

Think Tank: 38,292.4 miles

Data Place: 1. 6.3 oz **2.** 9.8 oz **3.** croquet **4.** no **5.** table tennis ball

Puzzler: 162; 4; 40; no, there will be two leftover students.

Jumpstart 14

Number Place: (Left to right) 30,900,000; 92,807.05; 1,286,000.4; 4,000,041,000; 8,726,739.03; 5,528,910,000

Fast Math: (Left to right) 800; 156; 1.9; 0.625; <, >, >

Think Tank: 57.6 ft

Data Place: Sample graph:

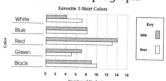

Answers will vary; sample answer: In general, the difference between colors boy and girls chose is not very great.

Puzzler: Biscuit; all Finn's preferred foods end in consonants.

Jumpstart 15

Number Place: (Left to right) 0.05; 10; 0.009; 40; 7,000; 0.005
Fast Math: 0.03; 0.011; 0.15; 25
Think Tank: 9.12 km
Data Place:

Player	Hits	At-bats	Batting Average
Jackson	5	40	.125
Ruiz	27	90	.300
Morita	46	184	.250
Hunter	48	120	.400
Sullivan	26	60	.433

1. Morita **2.** Hunter **3.** 9
Puzzler: 1. 137 – 84 **2.** 78 × 43 + 1
3. 48 × 371

Jumpstart 16

Number Place: 0.6834; 124.755
Fast Math: (Left to right) 7; 1; 8; 9; 7; 45
Think Tank: 7.249 m
Data Place: 1. 5 **2.** 4 **3.** 1 **4.** 11
Puzzler:

1. **2.**

Jumpstart 17

Number Place: (Left to right) 8; 5; 6; 3; 1; 13; 12 and 18; there are none.
Fast Math: (Left to right) 9; 3; 13; 3; 8; 0
Think Tank: $2\frac{7}{8}$ lb
Data Place: 1. 80 **2.** Wednesday and Thursday **3.** 235 **4.** They are declining.
5. Answers may vary; sample answers: A new pizza store opened nearby; there was bad weather.

Puzzler:

$1\frac{2}{3}$	$\frac{3}{4}$	$1\frac{1}{6}$	$1\frac{7}{12}$
$1\frac{1}{2}$	$1\frac{1}{4}$	$\frac{2}{3}$	$1\frac{3}{4}$
$\frac{11}{12}$	$1\frac{5}{6}$	$1\frac{5}{12}$	1
$1\frac{1}{12}$	$1\frac{1}{3}$	$1\frac{11}{12}$	$\frac{5}{6}$

Jumpstart 18

Number Place: (Left to right) 12; 10; 80; 60; 60; 360; 56; 135; 104
Fast Math: (Left to right) $\frac{1}{2}$; $\frac{7}{12}$; $7\frac{3}{8}$; $\frac{3}{40}$; $1\frac{7}{8}$; $2\frac{3}{4}$; $1\frac{23}{24}$; $28\frac{11}{18}$
Think Tank: Greater than; as terms increase and the difference stays the same, the value of the fraction increases.
Data Place: 1. 1 **2.** 8 **3.** 2 **4.** 36–40; it is the tallest bar.
Puzzler: 1. 12.56, 1.08 **2.** 31.2, 19.4
3. 15.5, 2.5

Jumpstart 19

Number Place: (Left to right) 0; 1; $\frac{1}{2}$; $\frac{1}{2}$; 0; $\frac{1}{2}$; $\frac{1}{2}$; $\frac{1}{2}$; answers may vary; sample answers: $\frac{5}{11}$; $\frac{7}{15}$; $\frac{9}{18}$; $\frac{5}{9}$; $\frac{13}{27}$; $\frac{4}{8}$; $\frac{10}{21}$; $\frac{15}{30}$
Fast Math: (Left to right) $\frac{1}{2}$; $\frac{1}{6}$; 12; $14\frac{2}{3}$; 50; $1\frac{1}{4}$

Jumpstart 20

Think Tank: $19\frac{1}{8}$ ft³
Data Place: 1. $14.00 **2.** No; she'll be $1.40 short. **3.** tadpole taco with special pond sauce, 1 drink, 1 dessert
Puzzler: 66 handshakes

Jumpstart 20

Number Place: (Left to right) 100; 10,000; 1,100; 3,000; 1,000,000; 10,025
Fast Math: (Left to right) $13\frac{1}{3}$; $9\frac{1}{2}$; 32; 5; $6\frac{1}{4}$; 8,000; <; =; =; <; <; <
Think Tank: $1\frac{1}{2}$ min
Data Place: 1. 48 **2.** 6 **3.** $\frac{15}{48}$ or $\frac{5}{16}$ **4.** $\frac{36}{48}$ or $\frac{3}{4}$ **5.** fourth and seventh
Puzzler: Pair off numbers to make sums of 101; 101 × 50 = 5,050

Jumpstart 21

Number Place: 5,999,999,998; 1,000,499,999
Fast Math: (Left to right) 0.06; 9,700; 480; 19,000; 768; 0.621; =; >; >; >; =; >
Think Tank: City A because 145 cm > 139.5 cm
Data Place: 1. 9.4; $32.81 **2.** 19.3; $59.64 **3.** $29.53
Puzzler: The stack would reach about one mile in height.

Jumpstart 22

Number Place: >; <; >; >
Fast Math: (Left to right) 2; 4; 2; 1; $1\frac{1}{20}$; $\frac{5}{8}$; $\frac{2}{3}$; 4; $\frac{6}{11}$
Think Tank: $333\frac{1}{3}$ pounds
Data Place: 1. $6.68 **2.** $7.06
Puzzler: 1. 7 **2.** 11

Jumpstart 23

Number Place: Answers may vary; sample answers: $3y$; $7b$; $m-6$; $\frac{x}{4}$; $p+10$
Fast Math: (Left to right) 21; 45; $\frac{1}{90}$; 16; $10\frac{1}{2}$; $2\frac{2}{3}$; $2\frac{1}{6}$; $2\frac{2}{5}$; 4
Think Tank: 63
Data Place: 1. I, II, III **2.** (1, 6), (5, –2), (6, 2) **3.** Boxer, IV
Puzzler: Answers may vary; sample answer:

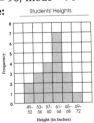

Jumpstart 24

Number Place: $x = 0.3$; $z = 1.85$
Fast Math: (Left to right) 11, 8, 8, 8; 34, 60, 59, no mode
Think Tank: range = 12; mean = about 89; median = 90; mode = 90
Data Place:

Students' Heights

Jumpstart 24 (continued)

Puzzler: 3.7 + 4.6 = 8.3; 1.9 + 3.0 = 4.9; 2.3 + 4.9 = 7.2

Jumpstart 25

Number Place: –6, –4; –8, –2
Fast Math: (Left to right) $.88, $2.42, $2.35, $2.35; $2\frac{7}{8}$, $1\frac{27}{40}$, $1\frac{1}{8}$, no mode
Think Tank: 296–297
Data Place: 1. F **2.** D **3.** C **4.** B **5.** D
Puzzler: The 7-lb bag has tea.

Jumpstart 26

Number Place: –5; +400; –75; +6
Fast Math: $n + 7$; $n - 2.8$; $n^2 + 8$; $12n$
Think Tank: $40.00
Data Place: Questions will vary; sample questions: **1.** On which two days did Mia run a total of 7 km? **2.** How much farther did Mia run on Monday than on Sunday? **3.** What is the difference between her longest and shortest runs?
Puzzler: The line segment is a chord crossing from between 9 and 10 to between 3 and 4. The sum on each side of the chord is 39.

Jumpstart 27

Number Place: $n > 3$; $n \geq -2$
Fast Math: $2n + 3$; $3n - 4^2$; $2n - 5$; $2.5n + 8.5$; $45n^2$
Think Tank: $10 + d$
Data Place:

Shoe Size	Tally	Frequency
5	I	1
7	I	1
8	IIII I	5
9	IIII I	6
10	IIII	4
11	IIII	4
12	III	3
14	I	1

Summaries will vary.
Puzzler: 9

Jumpstart 28

Number Place: $m \geq -1$; $m < -4$
Fast Math: (Left to right) 7; 22; 3; 14; 1; 11; 27.5; 4; 5
Think Tank: $\frac{145.5}{y}$
Data Place: Sample graph:

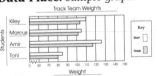

1. Find the greatest difference between start and finish weights. **2.** For each person, divide the total weight lost by the start weight. The greatest quotient matches the person who had lost the greatest fraction of his or her start weight.
Puzzler:

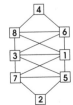

Jumpstart 29

Number Place: (Left to right) 0.9; $^6/_{100}$; $^{19}/_{1,000}$; 0.05; 1.003; $-4\,^1/_{100}$; $-^{14}/_{1,000}$; $2\,^3/_{10,000}$
Fast Math: (Left to right) 10.81; 5.62; 0.61; 6.37; 3.24; 0.89
Think Tank: Tuesday
Data Place: 1. 3:30 P.M., 5:30 P.M., 6:30 P.M. **2.** 4:00 A.M., 6:00 A.M., 5:00 A.M. **3.** 8:15 P.M., 5:15 P.M., 7:15 P.M.
Puzzler:

Jumpstart 30

Number Place: $-9, -6, -5, -2; -40, -4, 4, 40; 19, 9, -9, -91; 17, 7, -17, -77$
Fast Math: (Left to right) $5n; 3n; 7n; 7n - 3s; 9y + 2; 12t$
Think Tank: $60
Data Place: Check students' grids. **1.** $A'(3, 7); B'(3, -3)$ **2.** translation; right 1 unit, down 2 units
Puzzler: $31.20

Jumpstart 31

Number Place: (Left to right) $^{12}/_{20}$, $^5/_{20}$; $^9/_{10}$, $^4/_{10}$; $^{35}/_{60}$, $^{36}/_{60}$; $<$; $<$; $=$
Fast Math: $w + 2.5 = 3.8; y - 82 = 47;$ $^n/_{0.5} = 2; ^3/_8 k = 1\,^7/_8$
Think Tank: 180 miles
Data Place: 1. 23 **2.** 21 **3.** 8 stories **4.** between 11 and 22 **5.** 22 stories
Puzzler: 1. $^9/_{21}$, any fraction $= ^3/_8$ **2.** $1\,^{11}/_{18}$, any number equivalent to $1\,^5/_9$

Jumpstart 32

Number Place: $^5/_8, ^5/_6, ^6/_7, ^7/_8; ^3/_{10}, ^3/_8, ^1/_2, ^3/_5;$ $^{10}/_7, 1\,^1/_7, 1, ^7/_{10}; 2\,^3/_4, 2\,^2/_3, 2\,^1/_2, 2\,^2/_5$
Fast Math: (Left to right) $n = 135; m = 16; b = 99; y = 13; t = 14; n = 311$
Think Tank: 14 bugs
Data Place: 1. Wynn Field, 48,000 **2.** Clark Park **3.** Wynn Field **4.** Clark Park **5.** 11,280
Puzzler: $P = 32$ units; $A = 64$ square units

Jumpstart 33

Number Place: (Left to right) $<$; $=$; $>$; $>$; $>$; $=$
Fast Math: (Left to right) $n = 20; w = 15;$ $y = 13,800; s = 1,800; m = 2.5; p = 8,450$
Think Tank: Multiply the weekly price by 52. Find the difference between the two total prices to determine the savings.
Data Place:

Quarter	1	2	3	4	Final Score
Modem	10	5	17	9	41
Drive	7	9	13	14	43

The Drive

Puzzler:

Jumpstart 34

Number Place: (Left to right) $<$; $>$; $>$; $<$; $<$; $>$
Fast Math: (Left to right) $n = 1.2; m = 26;$ $b = 2.36; y = 50; t = 3.4; r = 0.1017$
Think Tank: $3,382\,^1/_2$ ft³
Data Place: 1. yes **2.** The horizontal scale has been expanded in Graph B. **3.** Graph A
Puzzler: $3\,^1/_4 + 5\,^5/_8 = 9$

Jumpstart 35

Number Place: (Top to bottom) $-1.6, -1.2, 1.2, 1.6; -1\,^1/_2, -^1/_2, ^1/_2, 1;$ $-10.01, -10, 10, 10.1; -2\,^1/_4, -2, 2, 2\,^1/_4$
Fast Math: (Left to right) $n = 1\,^7/_{10};$ $m = ^5/_8; b = ^{13}/_{14}; y = 7\,^3/_8; t = 1\,^2/_5; k = 2\,^1/_2$
Think Tank: 10; 55
Data Place: 1. 3 **2.** 2 **3.** 69 **4.** 26 **5.** 54 **6.** 7
Puzzler: 47

Jumpstart 36

Number Place: $400, 85, 145,405; 92, 164, 65,408; 330, 132, 12,408$
Fast Math: (Left to right) $n = 152; m = 18\,^2/_3; b = 1\,^1/_8; w = ^4/_7; t = 2\,^1/_{12}; p = 10$
Think Tank: $^1/_9$
Data Place:

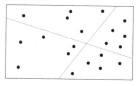

Puzzler:

Jumpstart 37

Number Place: (Left to right) $3, 9; 2, 5, 10; 2, 3, 4, 6, 8; 2, 3, 5, 6, 9, 10; 2, 3, 4, 5, 6, 10$
Fast Math: (Left to right) $5; -2; 4; 10; 0; -15; -4; -8; -4$
Think Tank: 14 ft²
Data Place:

Stem	Leaf
4	7
5	4 5 9 9
6	2 2 2 6
7	0 3
8	2 2

1. 35 **2.** 62 **3.** 62 **4.** median
Puzzler: The answer should be the original integer.

Jumpstart 38

Number Place: c, p, c, p, p; false, 2 is an even prime number; false, $2 + 3 = 5$
Fast Math: (Left to right) $8; -40; 126;$ $-250; 0; 96; -40; 48; -42$
Think Tank: $-1°C$
Data Place: 1. mean, 69.3 **2.** mode, 90 **3.** median, 63
Puzzler: 1. no; figure would have $> 180°$ **2.** yes **3.** yes **4.** no; figure would have $< 360°$

Jumpstart 39

Number Place: (Left to right) 326; 15; 18; 4.5; $^2/_5$; 0.6; 22; 0; 87; $^5/_8$
Fast Math: (Left to right) $5\,^1/_2; 1\,^3/_8; 5\,^1/_3;$ $1\,^1/_4; 0; -9; -4.7; -^2/_5; ^1/_{12}$
Think Tank: 0.5 days
Data Place:

x	$x + 0.5$	(x, y)
0	0.5	(0, 0.5)
1	1.5	(1, 1.5)
2	2.5	(2, 2.5)
3	3.5	(3, 3.5)
4	4.5	(4, 4.5)
5	5.5	(5, 5.5)

Check students' graphs; yes; the graph is a straight line.
Puzzler: 7:00; 1:30; 9:25

Jumpstart 40

Number Place: (Left to right) $2^3 = 8; 2^2 \times 3^3 = 108; 3^4 \times 4 = 324; 5^3 \times 12 = 1,500; 3^2 \times 4^3 = 576; 6^2 \times 2^2 = 144$
Fast Math: Answers may vary; (Left to right) any number > 9; any number < -21; any number < -5; any number ≤ -1; any number > 2; any number ≤ -4
Think Tank: 1:50 A.M.
Data Place: 1. Negative correlation; the temperature drops as the time gets later. **2.** 4:00 P.M. to 8:00 P.M.
Puzzler: 40

Jumpstart 41

Number Place: (Left to right) $<$; $>$; $=$; $>$; $>$; $<$; $>$; $>$; $<$
Fast Math: (Left to right) 1 to 3; 2 : 5; $^1/_3$; 2 to 3; 5 : 3; 2 to 1; 4 : 1; $^1/_7$; 3 to 5; 2 : 1
Think Tank: 4 to 3; 4 to 9
Data Place: 1. 20% **2.** 28% **3.** 68% **4.** 100% **5.** 76% **6.** 140%
Puzzler:

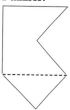

Jumpstart 42

Number Place: (Left to right) 2^3; 2^5; 5^3; 2×5^2; $2^2 \times 3 \times 5$; $2^5 \times 3$

Fast Math: (Top to bottom) 9 to 6, 36 : 24; 20 : 14, 1 to 0.7; 9 to 5

(Left to right) $\neq$; =; =; $\neq$; =; =

Think Tank: 12

Data Place:

Item	Gil's Grocery	Mira's Market	Fiona's Foods
Corn Muffin	4 for $6	10 for $18	**5 for $7.40**
Yogurt	4 for $3.40	6 for $4.62	**5 for $3.75**
Canned Tuna	6 for $7.50	4 for $4.88	**5 for $6.00**

Puzzler:

Object	Top View	Front View	Side View
(cylinder)	(circle)	(rectangle)	(rectangle)
(rectangular solid)	(square)	(bracket)	(bracket)

Jumpstart 43

Number Place: Answers will vary; sample answers: (Left to right) $\frac{2}{4}$; $\frac{4}{8}$; $\frac{6}{10}$; $\frac{9}{15}$; $-\frac{6}{16}$; $-\frac{9}{24}$; $1\frac{2}{4}$; $1\frac{10}{20}$; $-3\frac{4}{10}$; $-3\frac{8}{20}$; $5\frac{6}{20}$, $5\frac{9}{30}$; $-\frac{2}{8}$; $-\frac{3}{12}$; $-\frac{4}{14}$; $-\frac{6}{21}$; $-3\frac{14}{16}$; $-3\frac{21}{24}$

Fast Math: (Left to right) 7 mph; 1 for $7; 8 ft/sec; 1 for $3.50; 1.5 pages/min; 1 can for $.60

Think Tank: 600 doses

Data Place:

Player	Years	Won	Lost
Lefty Lebowitz	1988–1990	42	14
Hands Hansen	1997–1999	**48**	16
Stringbean Gomez	2004–2006	36	**12**
Baby Face Jonas	2008–2010	**33**	11
Big Mo Tanaka	2012–	15	**5**

18 games

Puzzler: (Top to bottom)

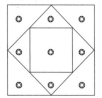

Jumpstart 44

Number Place: (Left to right) $\frac{1}{2}$; $\frac{4}{5}$; $\frac{1}{6}$; $-\frac{4}{7}$; $-\frac{5}{8}$; $-\frac{2}{9}$; $-\frac{1}{5}$; $1\frac{3}{4}$; $1\frac{2}{5}$; $-2\frac{7}{9}$

Fast Math: (Left to right) yes; no; no; no; yes; yes; no; no; yes

Think Tank: 7 ft

Data Place: Answers may vary; sample answers: **1.** 1 circle to 2 triangles **2.** 2 triangles to total number of figures **3.** 1 circle to 6 polygons **4.** 3 quadrilaterals to 1 hexagon **5.** 2 triangles to 3 quadrilaterals

Puzzler:

Jumpstart 45

Number Place: (Left to right) $1\frac{5}{7}$; $2\frac{2}{3}$; $-2\frac{2}{3}$; $4\frac{1}{2}$; $-1\frac{2}{3}$; $-\frac{5}{4}$; $\frac{67}{20}$; $\frac{22}{9}$; $\frac{19}{3}$; $-\frac{29}{13}$

Fast Math: (Left to right) 15; 3; 13; 2; 56; 30; 36; 14; 3

Think Tank: 6 in

Data Place: 1. $75 **2.** January **3.** $79 **4.** March

Puzzler:

Object	Top View	Front View	Side View
(house shape)	(top view)	(front view)	(side view)
(diamond)	(pyramid)	(triangle)	(triangle)

Jumpstart 46

Number Place: (Left to right) -0.7; $-\frac{3}{50}$; $\frac{1}{25}$; -0.03; -7.8; $-44\frac{11}{20}$; $-\frac{7}{500}$; 61.125

Fast Math: (Left to right) $\frac{7}{10}$; $\frac{1}{20}$; $\frac{16}{25}$; $1\frac{1}{2}$; $\frac{19}{20}$; $2\frac{1}{4}$; $\frac{3}{25}$; $1\frac{6}{25}$; 40%; 87.5%; 80%; 62.5%; 160%; 4%; 7%; 125%

Think Tank: 6 cm

Data Place: 1. 32% **2.** 16% **3.** 40% **4.** 12% **5.** 40% **6.** 76%

Puzzler: Player 1

Jumpstart 47

Number Place: (Left to right) $r - 1$; $\frac{n}{7}$; $\frac{1}{4}y$ or $\frac{y}{4}$; $k + m$; $\frac{n}{8}$; $5t$; $\frac{60}{x}$

Fast Math: (Left to right) 0.4; 0.08; 0.01; 0.115; 2.16; 0.007; 0.003; 1.25; 20%; 2%; 87.5%; 350%; 180%; 7%; 125%; 99.5%

Think Tank: 60 in or 5 ft tall

Data Place: 1. 130 **2.** 75 **3.** 105 **4.** 115 **5.** 95

Puzzler: 31.25%

Jumpstart 48

Number Place: (Left to right) 6; -8.5; $3\frac{1}{2}$; 0.04; 12; $-4\frac{1}{4}$; 3.5; 1.007; -32; -53; 3.05; $\frac{3}{8}$

Fast Math: (Left to right) 10; 9; 20; 8; 2; 5; =; >

Think Tank: 20%

Data Place: 1. yes **2.** $\frac{1}{2}$ **3.** $\frac{2}{3}$ **4.** $\frac{1}{12}$ **5.** $\frac{7}{12}$ **6.** $\frac{1}{6}$ **7.** $\frac{1}{6}$

Puzzler: 1. T **2.** F **3.** T **4.** F

Jumpstart 49

Number Place: commutative; associative; identity; identity; distributive

Fast Math: (Left to right) 60%; 50%; 25%; 80%; 9.2%; 250%

Think Tank: 135

Data Place: 1. *DB, CE* **2.** *FE, FB, FC, FD* **3.** Answers may vary; sample answers: *EBF, FBC, EBC* **4.** Answers may vary; sample answers: *BDC, ADB, ADC* **5.** *ADFE* **6.** *CFB*

Puzzler: Answers may vary; sample answer: Cross first with sister; leave her there; return for brother; leave brother and bring back sister; drop off sister, pick up cake, take it across and leave with brother; go back to bring sister across

Jumpstart 50

Number Place: Answers may vary; sample answers: rounded; rounded; exact; exact; exact

Fast Math: (Left to right) 90; 72; 384; 45; 2,500; 800

Think Tank: $\frac{2}{3}$; 0

Data Place: Answers may vary; sample answers: **1.** bar **2.** circle **3.** line **4.** histogram

Puzzler: Step 1: Put three coins in each pan to weigh them. Step 2: Weigh any two coins from the lighter pan. The fake coin is the lighter coin; if the pans are in balance, the fake is the third coin.